Bring on Goliath

Lemon Law Justice in America

Bring on Goliath
Lemon Law Justice in America

Vince Megna

Ken Press

TUCSON

In loving memory of my Mother,

Lorraine M. Megna

Published by Ken Press, Tucson, Arizona USA

(520) 743-3200 or office@kenpress.com

Copyright ©2004 by Vince Megna

Printed in Canada.

Megna, Vince

Bring on Goliath : lemon law justice in America / Vince Megna.—Tucson,
Ariz. : Ken Press, 2004.

p. ; cm.

Includes state by state rating of lemon laws.
ISBN: 1-928771-16-5

1. Automobile industry and trade—Law and legislation—United States—Popular
works. 2. Automobiles—Defects—Law and legislation—United States—Popular works.
3. Automobiles—Standards—United States—Popular works. 4. Consumer complaints—
United States—Popular works. 5. Consumer protection—United States—Popular works.
6. Quality of products—United States—Popular works. I. Title. II. Lemon law justice in
America.

KF2036.A8 M44 2004   2003109297
343.7309/44—dc22   0401

Prologue

I don't give a shit if they take
it or not. If the plaintiff doesn't
settle, it doesn't matter to us. We
tell them, "We're coming after you."

— **James A. Brown**
Assistant General Counsel
The Ford Motor Company
National Law Journal
March 18, 1996

I get to my office around 10:00 a.m. sharp. I check with our receptionist Sharon for messages and see if anything is on the seat cushion of my custom leatherette "executive" chair. All emergencies or urgent matters somehow find their way to this chair. Then, I walk downstairs hoping to find a cold Diet Coke in the refrigerator. Nothing else will do. I won't drink Pepsi, Mountain Dew or some 10 percent real fruit flavored non-carbonated punch. With Coke in hand, I return to my office to see what major manufacturer will be sued next. This, typically, is how my day begins.

Mid-March 1996 was no exception. When I returned to my office with the first Diet of the day, I noticed that the new *National Law Journal*, a weekly newspaper for the legal profession, had arrived. The front page caught my eye. Some arrogant looking SOB was pictured in white shirt and black tie, with arms folded, standing abrasively in front of a blue Mustang convertible. The caption read, "Lean, Mean Litigation Machine — Ford Thinks It Has A Better Idea: Hardball."

The individual that I had judged an arrogant bastard was none other than James A. Brown, assistant general counsel at Ford Motor Company and manager of product liability litigation. Mr. Brown was delivering a message on behalf of the High and Mighty Detroit Giant to plaintiffs' attorneys and the clients they serve. The crux of the message was simple. Ford had changed its corporate attitude from "Screw you," to "Fuck you."

Mr. Brown would lead the charge against victims injured by defective Ford products. Cases would no longer be settled based on merit. The Giant would try any case, no matter how small, no matter how great the risk of a mammoth jury verdict, just to scare other victims and their lawyers from filing suit. The message was clear: "If you sue Ford, be ready for war." And, as part of the battle cry, plaintiffs were offered a one-time, take-it-or-leave-it, low-ball settlement. If they took it, fine; Ford got off cheap. If they rejected it, Mr. Brown's zealous statement on the front page of the *Journal* eloquently summed up Ford's compassion for the injured.

"I don't give a shit if they take it or not. If the plaintiff doesn't settle, it doesn't matter to us. We tell them, 'We're coming after you.'"

For over a decade, I've been fighting Giants. I'm a Lemon Law lawyer practicing out of Waukesha, Wisconsin. I represent people who buy cars and trucks and suffer for it. My track record is good. In fact, it's more than good. I'm one of the best in the country. Out of more than 1,000 cases in 13 years, I've lost 9. But on this day, I didn't file any lawsuits. I didn't write any letters to Dearborn, Michigan. I didn't make any phone calls to GM's attorneys, Bowman & Brooke, in Minneapolis. What I did do was more important.

I took the *Journal*, got in my car and drove to Creative Enterprise, my brother-in-law's wholesale framing business. I waited three hours while one of the most disheartening stories I had ever read was double matted and framed.

Today, the Attorney Brown Hardball article hangs in my office as a continuous reminder of the Almighty Industry we fight and the true corporate greed that permeates our society.

Contents

Lemon Law

Laws passed in all 50 states and
the District of Columbia to give
legal recourse to consumers
who buy or lease vehicles that
have ongoing mechanical
or other problems.

We call these vehicles lemons.

The Showroom

There is so much bullshit out there, you need a shovel just to get past 12 noon.

— Vince Megna

I hate buying new cars. I hate entering the showroom. I hate talking to salespeople. I don't want to hear about the fabulous deal that ends tonight at 9:00 or how the rebate is only good through the end of the month or how two other people are interested in the same car that caught my eye or how rustproofing and paint protection will extend the life of my new car.

I don't want to be told that the advertised specials have all been sold or that I can get $1,000 in trade for my lawnmower. I don't want my salesperson to claim that I'm buying below invoice or that the dealership is losing money. I know I'm getting screwed. I'm buying a new car! I just don't want my picture pinned to the bulletin board as last month's customer who "took it up the butt." I'd like to retain some sense of dignity as a new car purchaser.

The reputation for fraud, double-dealing and deception was not simply bestowed on the auto industry as a whole; it was earned... one customer at a time. Since the first odometer rollback, through last week's 27.9 percent APR finance contract, the industry has taken great pride in being master of the flimflam. "I'll say anything for a sale," remains the battle cry of the sales executive and it all begins the moment you set foot on the showroom floor.

I'll Say Anything

I want you to know about my first experience on the "showroom floor." It happened in a warehouse furniture store, not a car dealership, but the same principles apply.

I was a third year law student looking for living room furniture. I researched various brand names. I couldn't afford the best. But I didn't want "Daewoo," either. My investigation showed that a company named Bassett made decent, affordable furniture.

I went to a warehouse-type store that carried low to medium priced furniture. As soon as I opened the door, it began.

"My name is Hal. I'll be your salesman. How can I help you?"

I told Hal what I needed and asked whether he carried Bassett.

"Of course we do," he replied. "It's one of the finest lines on the market."

Great, I thought. On a scale of one to ten, Bassett is a four and this guy's telling me it's top of the line. If it were top of the line, it wouldn't be HERE. I love sales. I love salesmen.

Hal walked me through the store. I saw more three-piece living room groupings than any individual should see in a lifetime. I liked the three-piece idea — sofa, chair, loveseat — but it was too expensive. The lawyer money wouldn't start rolling in for another year. I had to go cheaper. Hal showed me a brown four-piece sectional that would work. I asked if Bassett was the manufacturer. In true salesman form, he responded, "Yes, it is." We had a deal.

Hal wrote up a contract and asked me to sign. In law school they suggested reading contracts before signing. So, I did. The sectional was described as Gaines. Bassett didn't appear anywhere on the contract. I asked Hal about this.

"Bassett owns Gaines," he said. "This is a Gaines/Bassett

piece." He then wrote Bassett on the contract next to the word Gaines and we closed the deal.

My new Gaines/Bassett sectional arrived flawed. The corner section was much darker than the other sections. More importantly, away from the showroom lighting, this was very ugly, very cheap furniture. I had gotten the Daewoo after all. Thankfully, I had studied the Uniform Commercial Code — a consumer protection law. Because the corner section didn't match, I could reject these goods. I could ask for a refund. I served the store with a UCC "Notice of Rejection" demanding my money back. At the same time, I checked into the Gaines/Bassett issue.

I found that Gaines and Bassett were two separate companies, completely unrelated. The good people at Bassett even sent a letter to that effect. I had Hal now. He had lied to me. Fraud. Misrepresentation. Punitive damages! My legal education was going to pay off, even before graduation. There was no such furniture as Gaines/Bassett.

When your opponent is down, make sure he stays down. When I went back to the store, I took a witness. I wanted Hal to tell me again that my sectional was Gaines/Bassett. My witness would then sign an affidavit to that effect as proof of misrepresentation. The great thing about salespeople is that they never admit a lie. They just keep huffing and puffing. Hal reassured me that the furniture I bought was manufactured by Bassett under the trade name Gaines. He went on to tell me, "Gaines/Bassett is a well respected line of furniture." Yeah, I thought, about as well respected as your line of BS. Still, I was pleased. My case was solidified. I had a witness. They would pay.

The store owners invited me in to discuss the matter. I explained how I had been defrauded, how Hal had misrepresented the product, how I was screwed. I offered to settle for a sofa, chair, loveseat combination of my choosing. They chuckled and advised, "This isn't the way to start a law career."

In response, I pointed to a three-piece grouping that was acceptable to me. Since it cost nearly three times as much as my original Gaines/Bassett, I gave them a break — they wouldn't have to deliver — I would pick it up myself.

I said, "If this is not agreeable, I'll sue. You'll be my first case."

I'd have to wait for that first case. They agreed, reluctantly, and my living room finally had some furniture.

The Numbers Don't Lie

A friend of mine in the retail music store business once told me, "The numbers don't lie." Obviously, he was unfamiliar with the accounting firm of Arthur Anderson, LLP or the automobile industry.

Americans spend, on average, 20 percent of their after-tax income on new cars. Some, like Audrey T., spend even more. Audrey ran a small daycare center in Milwaukee's central city. Occasionally, she gave rides to the children. Safe and reliable transportation was a must. The KIA Sportage was affordable, less than $14,000 according to television ads, and came with a 100,000 mile warranty. The Yellow Pages directed her to the local, "Save a Fist Full of Dollars," dealer.

A beaming salesman introduced himself and showed Audrey a fully equipped KIA Sportage with a Manufacturer's Suggested Retail Price (MSRP) of $19,815. Audrey felt the price was too high and asked to see the advertised specials.

"The TV cars are stripped down models," she was told. "They won't serve your purpose. In the business, we call them 'lost leaders.'" With a wink and a smile, the salesman assured her that he could put her in the "loaded" KIA.

After a short discussion about financing, it was apparent that Audrey would not qualify for the purchase. She had $300 cash and questionable credit. Even with the $1,000 rebate being offered, no lending institution would write this deal. The new KIA was simply beyond her means. That never stopped a car salesman. Illusion is the foundation of the auto industry.

The Sportage shown to Audrey listed at $19,815. As a rule, KIAs don't sell for list price. They are almost always discounted. The "Fist Full of Dollars" dealer was happy to subtract $2,245 from the MSRP, bringing the selling price to $17,570. After Audrey put down $300 in cash and signed over the $1,000 rebate, she would need to borrow $16,270. Another problem. That $1,300 total down payment was only 7.4 percent of the purchase price, too low for a down payment. There would not be enough equity in the car. In the banking world, the "debt to equity ratio" would be too high, especially for someone with questionable credit. The deal would fall through. It was time for dealer magic.

Instead of discounting the Sportage $2,245, the salesman ADDED $955 to the MSRP. He wrote a contract indicating the selling price as $20,770. Audrey would still make the same $1,300 down payment. So far it looked like she owed $19,470. If she couldn't get a loan for $16,270, how was this deal going to fly? Oh, it would fly.

The salesman flat out lied on the installment contract. He showed that Audrey put down $3,500 in cash, instead of $300. This $3,200 of phony money was created — made from nothing. Audrey's total down payment now appeared to be $4,500, or 21.6 percent of the selling price. The debt to equity ratio was fine. A loan in the amount of $16,270 ($20,770 minus the $4,500) was obtained.

Creative Sales Technique
Used in Getting Audrey Financing

Honest Numbers		Deceptive Numbers	
KIA Sportage MSRP	$19,815	KIA Sportage MSRP	$19,815
Normal discount	−$2,245	"Arbitrary" increase	+$955
Normal selling price	**$17,570**	**Inflated selling price**	**$20,770**
Manufacturer's rebate	$1,000	Manufacturer's rebate	$1,000
Audrey's down payment	+$300	Audrey's down payment	+$300
		Fabricated down payment *(equals the difference between the normal and inflated selling prices)*	**+$3,200**
Total down payment	**$1,300**	**Total down payment** (includes fictitious **$3,200**)	**$4,500**
Total amount of bank loan ($17,570 − $1,300)	$16,270	Total amount of bank loan ($20,770 − $4,500)	$16,270
Percentage of down payment compared to selling price ($1,300 ÷ $17,570 x 100)	**7.4%**	Percentage of down payment compared to selling price ($4,500 ÷ $20,770 x 100)	**21.6%**

*The lender **would not approve** Audrey's loan because of her questionable credit and the low down payment percentage.*

*The lender **did approve** Audrey's loan with this greater down payment percentage.*

The abuse didn't stop. Audrey's interest rate was 26.5 percent. Her monthly payments were $535.57 for 60 months. Interest was $14,612.58. Total payments came to $32,134.20. Tony Soprano and Uncle Junior would have been proud to carry this paper.

Fortunately, KIA has never won any blue ribbons. The loaded Sportage had bad brakes. Audrey became my client and the KIA was bought back under the Lemon Law. Her nightmare was ended.

The Trade-in

Car dealers also play tricks with trades. They create equity when none exists. They claim to give thousands of dollars for crap at the annual Push, Pull or Drag Sale. And, if you hit one of those special Saturdays, you can get a $1,000 trade-in allowance for that broken-down lawnmower that's been sitting in your garage for 15 years. Here are a couple of examples of trading for your dollars.

A guy with no ready cash wants to use his trade-in as a down payment on a new car. He owes $14,000 on the trade. He visits a dealer and finds a new car for $20,000. The trade is appraised at $14,000 — the exact amount he owes. Since he has no money and no equity, the deal appears doomed. However, Detroit earns nothing by turning customers away.

The dealer writes up a contract arbitrarily increasing the price of the new car to $24,000. The trade-in allowance is then bumped to $18,000. By manipulation, $4,000 of equity has been artificially created. The buyer now has his down payment. The deal will fly.

Another similar trade-in trick involves the over-allowance. This is most effective with a customer who is intent on getting top dollar in trade but is not aware that most new vehicles can be discounted 8 to 12 percent with a little negotiation.

In pulling this off, the dealership simply does not discount the purchase price. Instead, the trade-in allowance is increased. That's all there is to it. Once again, the bottom line remains pretty much the same, but the buyer thinks he's getting a great deal — thousands more for the trade-in. And when we think it's a great deal, we can't pass it up.

The Demo

Demonstrators aren't new cars, but they're not really used either. They're hybrids. Key dealership personnel take new cars as perks, drive them for a few thousand miles and then put them on the lot as demos. Still, the demo will be more expensive than the typical used or pre-owned vehicle. Dealerships like to sell demos because they are low mileage and have never been privately titled. They can be pitched as "like new" and can be moved faster than the average used car.

My favorite demo story involves a couple we'll call Jack and Diane, two American kids out in the showroom "promised land." In 1999, they were ready to buy their first new car. They visited one of the most "reputable" Pontiac dealers in town and were greeted by a smiling sales executive we'll call Harry. He asked what they would like to drive home and how much they could afford.

Jack said, "We like the new Bonneville. We've saved $8,000 to put down." Harry's face lit up.

"This is your lucky day," he said. "I've got the perfect car, a black satin Bonneville demo with less than 5,000 miles. It was driven by one of our salesmen who lived in Green Bay. He commuted to work."

Harry explained that demos were "just like new," but cheaper. Still, Jack was a little concerned about the car. It wasn't new and it didn't cost that much less. He didn't want somebody else's trouble. Harry assured him that everything was okay.

"Ninety percent of the miles are highway driven, Green Bay to Milwaukee. Highway miles are good for a car. And besides," Harry went on, "you guys are young. Anytime you can save a buck, do it. You can't go wrong on this."

Somewhat hesitantly, Jack and Diane agreed to sit down and talk terms. Forty-five minutes later, my future clients signed a purchase contract. Harry just needed to get his manager's approval. He would be right back.

(Why do car salesmen always have to get approval? They know their cost for the car and how much they have to get. Why don't we just deal with the guy who gives the approval and cut out this fool? Then they couldn't play this game.)

While he was gone, another salesman stopped by. "What are you folks buying?"

Diane said, "The black Bonneville, the demo."

This salesman, obviously with an ax to grind, said, "I thought so. It's a nice car but it's no demo. That Bonne's a 'driver's ed' car."

Jack and Diane were stunned. The informant gave them a wink and was gone. A few minutes later, Harry was back with a grin from ear to ear.

"Congratulations. We've got a deal."

Diane was close to tears. She repeated the driver education story. In keeping with the Detroit spirit, Harry stuck to his guns.

"That's preposterous. Whoever you talked to is crazy. He doesn't know the first thing about that car. I know that car's history. Your Bonneville is a demonstrator. You have my word." Harry was convincing. That's his job. He sells cars. Jack and Diane believed him. They took delivery.

The cat stayed "in the bag" for a couple of weeks. Then, the title came. Attached was a notice indicating that the Bonneville HAD been used as a "driver's education vehicle." It was never a demo. Harry was a liar. Harry was a salesman. Why am I not surprised? Diane called my office.

We made Harry eat his words. We took the story to the dealer and told them, "Here's what it will take…."

Jack and Diane returned the demo for a brand new Bonneville with all the options of their choosing and the dealer paid the attorney fees. We won, but that was just one case. There's so much trickery going on out there, it's mind-boggling.

The Rebate — In Memory of John Riley

When John Riley walked into my office in January 1999, I noticed he and Warren Buffett had something in common — both drove Lincoln Town Cars. Mr. Buffett, one of the richest men in the world with a net worth of 30 billion dollars, owned a used 1994 model. Mr. Riley, a retired factory worker, leased a new 1998. He paid $15,777 up front for the privilege of driving a Lincoln for two years. Mr. Buffett, holder of 200 million shares of Coca-Cola, says a new car is a terrible investment. Mr. Riley was about to prove him wrong.

John Riley's Lincoln was a lemon. It pulled, didn't brake right, and wasn't fixed after numerous visits to the dealer. According to Wisconsin's Lemon Law, he was entitled to a refund. I sent a demand letter to my favorite automaker — Ford Motor Company. This time Ford was on the ball… almost.

About 30 days after my notice, Ford sent a check to Mr. Riley in the sum of $14,777. Why had they shortchanged him $1,000? I looked to Attorney Brown's picture hanging on my office wall for guidance.

"If the plaintiff doesn't settle, it doesn't matter to us. We tell them, 'We're coming after you.'"

I was inspired. I filed a lawsuit seeking double damages and attorney fees for John Riley.

Nothing much happened for about eight months. And then, just like in Perry Mason, the proverbial smoking gun surfaced in the form of an internal corporate memo. According to Ford, a $1,000 rebate was paid in the Riley transaction. Their records showed John put down $14,777 and applied a $1,000 manufacturer's rebate to equal a total lease price of $15,777. That was why Mr. Riley's refund was only $14,777. Ford thought that was all he had paid.

John assured me he did not get a rebate.

"Nothing was ever said about a rebate. No one at the dealership ever mentioned a rebate." John Riley had definitely paid $15,777.

I was beginning to get the picture. It wasn't Ford this time. It was the dealer. The dealer screwed John. The dealer kept the rebate. The dealer signed John's name on the rebate check and submitted it to Ford for payment. Mr. Riley was supposed to pay $14,777. Instead, he paid $15,777 and the dealer received $16,777. Ah, the free enterprise system at work. I was ready for trial.

Ford stipulated that the Lincoln was a lemon, but made the argument that Mr. Riley had received a full refund. Sometimes the brain of a giant is so small. We argued that John was flim-flammed, swindled — the mark of a con. The whole case hinged on one fact: whether or not John Riley had received a rebate.

It took the jury 20 minutes. Ford offered no witnesses, no testimony, no check, no endorsement, and no rebate. John Riley was awarded $31,165.56 plus costs. My office received $45,198.24 in attorney fees. Call me crazy, but wouldn't it have been cheaper just to pay John the $1,000 rebate?

Over a period of 26 months, John Riley made a profit of $15,388 on his $15,777 investment. In addition, he drove the Town Car for 24 months and 35,000 miles at no charge. Without adding any economic benefit enhancer for driving two free years, Mr. Riley's annual rate of return on investment was 45.01 percent per year. Warren Buffett views 20 percent as an excellent annual rate of return. Mr. Riley exceeded excellence by more than double. So Mr. Buffett would have to agree that the Riley Town Car lease turned out to be a phenomenal investment opportunity.

The Rustproof Package

In states with harsh winters, dealers push rustproof protection at the time of sale. They know it is worthless. Rustproofing doesn't work. It never has. It was worthless in 1960 and it is worthless today. Of course, in 1960, cars were rusting, so it made some sense to be concerned. However, it made no sense to believe that car dealers with spray guns could accomplish what Detroit couldn't, namely; applying a magical mist "undercoating" to your brand new automobile to eliminate rust. We are a gullible people. Rustproofing is nothing more than a modern day equivalent of the secret potion in the traveling medicine man's show.

Technological advancement has virtually eliminated rust problems in today's new cars. Metal sections of cars are dipped multiple times, like apples in taffy, in primer and anti-corrosion solutions before assembly. This multi-dip electrostatic application process ensures complete coating with five, six, seven or even eight layers of undercoat protection before finishing coats are applied. The factory process is certainly far superior to the lot boy with a spray can.

Even manufacturers are finally admitting that the rustproof package is a scam. Page 11 of General Motors' 2002 Chevrolet Warranty and Owner Assistance Information booklet reads as follows:

After-Manufacture Rustproofing

Your vehicle was built and designed to resist corrosion. Application of additional rust-inhibiting materials is neither necessary nor required under the Sheet Metal Coverage. GM makes no recommendation concerning the usefulness or value of such products.

Application of after-manufacture rustproofing products may actually create an environment which reduces the corrosion resistance built into your vehicle. Repairs to correct damage caused by such application are not covered under your GM New Vehicle Limited Warranty.

When the largest auto manufacturer in the world tells me that after-manufacturing rustproof protection is not necessary, that it may cause damage and will not be covered under warranty, I can take the hint.

Rustproofing is BULLSHIT! Stop buying it!

Liar Liar

The race for lowest scum in society has always been between the lawyer and the car salesman. Recently, the Catholic priest has thrown his collar into the competition. But that's another story.

Some years the lawyer comes out on the bottom, some years, the salesman. Either way, it's always a tight race. In the movie *Liar Liar*, Jim Carey played lawyer Fletcher Reede, a fast talking habitual liar. Through mystic intervention brought on by his five-year-old son's birthday wish, Reede is condemned to tell the truth, and only the truth, for one full day. With great difficulty, he does.

If I'd had a hand in writing *Liar Liar*, I would have had attorney Reede buckle under the extreme pressure of truthfulness and take his own life during the sixteenth hour. My script would have shown Mr. Carey making a suicide leap from the third-story ledge of a federal courthouse. The moral being, that 24 consecutive hours of nothing but the truth is too much to ask of any lawyer.

Now, if the role had been changed, if Jim Carey had played a car salesman, the truth would have sounded something like this:

"Good morning, ma'am. I've been selling cars on and off for 12 years. I've worked at 17 dealerships. I'm on straight commission. The more you pay, the more I make. Here we work on a rotation basis. That means I sit on my ass until it's my turn to take the next walk-in. It's that simple. It's the luck of the draw.

"I'll tell you something ma'am; I like the women. They're stupid. They don't know jack about cars and nothing about finance. I've sold more cars at sticker price to women than anybody at this dealership. And I'm proud of it. Damn proud!

"Now let's cut the crap. Let's get down to business. You came in to buy a car. I'm gonna sell you one. You're gonna feel pressure like you've never felt. I'll lie. I'll cheat. I'll do anything to make a deal. In 30 minutes, your name's gonna be on the dotted line. I'm gonna be in your purse. You'll wish you never got out of bed this morning. You'll wish you never saw my face. Now let's look at some cars.

"You see this Certified Used Chevy Tahoe? It's on its fourth transmission. It's a lemon, but you'll never know it. The lemon title brand has been removed. We call it laundering. That's right, for 50 bucks a pop some lowlife at the Department of Transportation washes titles clean. To us, it's just another quality used car.

"Now here's an American icon — the Ford Mustang. The sticker says low mileage. That's a lie. We rolled the odometer last week. We spun that baby for 20 minutes and dropped 25,000 miles. It's no big thing. There are 450,000 odometer roll-backs every year in the U.S. We just want our piece of the pie.

"Are you interested in a one-owner? Right now we don't have any. The three being advertised as one-owners are Budget rentals. It's all bullshit. We got 'em at auction. We say they're one-owners because we get more money. When you say "rental" the price goes down.

"This red Mitsubishi fell off the delivery truck. One of the chains broke. That bitch bounced like a beach ball. You get a new car warranty on this one and I'll guarantee you're gonna need it.

"That Dodge Stratus was hit twice. We never disclose prior damage. If you ask anybody around here if it was in an accident, we say no. Then, you try to prove otherwise.

"One thing about the dealership, it's all about money. The owner lives in a 12,000-square-foot shack overlooking Lake Michigan. He invites us up once a year to kiss his ass. If I didn't need this job, I'd tell them all where to go. But until I hit the lottery or meet some rich chick, I'm stuck selling cars to any loser who walks through those doors. And that's my take on the car business. I should have been a lawyer."

It's Just a Game

I'm Deck Shifflet, paralawyer.
My firm handles more car wrecks
than anybody in Memphis.
Insurance companies are terrified
of us.... We're going to get you
a bunch of money."

— The Rainmaker

In 1964, I was living in Los Angeles. I played guitar with Tommy Boyce and Bobby Hart before they wrote hit songs for the Monkees and sold 100 million records. Every Monday night we played a job in Santa Monica. I always took Sunset Boulevard to the club. Everything was there. The Whiskey A-Go-Go, the gigantic album-cover billboards, the dreamers and the hitchhikers. This was Hollywood and I was 20 years old.

One of those Monday nights I was sitting at a red light at the corner of Sunset and Fairfax, when all of a sudden, **BAM**. I got nailed from behind with the force of a freight train. I flew forward, and back, forward and back, forward and back again. I was dazed, almost knocked out. The driver of the other car got out shaking his head and apologizing. "Are you okay? I just didn't see you. I was looking for something on the front seat." The police came and filled out a report. We all went home.

The next day I woke up in excruciating pain and couldn't move my neck. I saw a doctor. I had whiplash, muscle spasm, bruises, contusions, contractions of my back. I was a personal injury case — the dream of every law school graduate. The good doctor scheduled me for unending physical therapy and referred me to an attorney I'll rename Jay Barker.

"Jay can get you money on this," I was told. Jay Barker was a pear shaped small-time LA ambulance chaser specializing in soft tissue injuries. Looking back, he reminds me of Danny DeVito scamming insurance money in *The Rainmaker*. But at the time, I was naive and in pain.

Mr. Barker was the consummate professional. The first thing he brought up was his fee. He was willing to take my case on a "contingency." This meant I didn't pay a fee unless we won. Some things never change. Today there is a TV ad playing every minute somewhere in this country with a lawyer begging, "No fee unless you win."

Under the agreement, Attorney Barker would get 40 percent of all monies recovered at trial or settlement and 50 percent if the case was appealed.

"That's a lot of my money," I thought. "This guy better be good." I signed the contract and continued therapy.

A few weeks later, I found out that the driver who rear-ended me was an uninsured, unemployed boxer. That didn't sound good. Most boxers don't make a lot of money. Unemployed boxers make even less. I talked to my lawyer.

"Don't worry about it," he said. "Half the people in LA don't have insurance. That's why you have Uninsured Motorist Coverage. We're going to collect on this one."

Barker explained that I would file a claim against my own insurance company. I couldn't sue in the traditional sense. There would be no judge, no jury. The case would be heard by an arbitrator in a "court of arbitration," something I would later learn to despise.

"Uninsured motorist arbitration claims are faster and less expensive than lawsuits. We've got a winner," I was assured.

A year later, I nervously attended my arbitration hearing. This was my first experience with the law since the police caught me throwing stones at light poles in the Milwaukee County Stadium parking lot after a Braves game. The arbitration went much worse than my father's reprimand. The arbitrator didn't believe I was hurt. My attorney didn't know the case and I was the only witness.

I was awarded $1,300, not 10 million like the woman who spilled coffee at McDonalds. After Jay took his 40 percent, there wasn't even enough money left to pay my medical bills. I still owed money. How could this happen? Why did I get almost nothing? I was injured — my neck still cracks to this day.

Attorney Barker had the answer. He offered this profound lawyerly insight — "It's just a game, son. Sometimes you win. Sometimes you lose. That's all there is to it."

It took a few seconds for his words to sink in. Then, my Sicilian blood started to boil. "No," I yelled back, "this isn't just a game. It's my case. You did a terrible job. The arbitrator was an idiot and I got screwed!"

On that smoggy southern California day, I lost a lot of respect for the legal system. The law shouldn't be a game. Lawyers shouldn't treat it like one. Bingo is a game. I started to seriously rethink my future.

Maybe the music business wasn't for me. I was doing well, playing with a lot of people on the brink of fame, but maybe my energy could be better directed. Maybe I should be a lawyer. I'd certainly do a better job than Jay Barker. I'd treat my clients with respect, never take their cases for granted, and never *ever* tell them, "It's just a game."

I decided to go back to school. If Rodney Dangerfield could do it, so could I. There was one small problem. My grades were poor. I had spent too much time in high school trying to play guitar like Herb Ellis. Back then, academia was not for me. Now, academia returned the compliment.

Every school I applied to rejected me and my future plans, including Marquette University in Milwaukee, my hometown. But Marquette rejected me with compassion. Their letter seemed to be more understanding. That's the Jesuits for you. I decided to try again. I spoke with Larry Giantomas, Assistant Dean of the College of Liberal Arts, about my dilemma. I told him I was much smarter than my grades indicated, that all I did in high school was play guitar and that if they'd give me a chance, I could do the work.

Dean Giantomas told me my transcript did not indicate college material. However, if I was serious, if I really wanted to get into Marquette, there was a way. I could attend the Milwaukee Institute of Technology, MIT, for a semester or two; take some general education courses. If I passed, I could transfer to Marquette. To this day, I am very appreciative for the guidance of Dean Giantomas.

MIT was no Harvard. It was a vocational/technical school that offered a few introductory college courses. High school dropouts earned GEDs. Beauticians learned to do hair. My uncle Sam called it "bums' college." My dad called it "barber school." To me, it was my opportunity to become a lawyer.

I met with my MIT admissions counselor, a man who was definitely in the wrong business. He told me I'd never make it at MIT. I wasn't cut out for higher education. I should apply at Briggs and Stratton for assembly line work. Nothing against the line, but I was going to be a lawyer.

I told Mr. Encouragement, "I have a pulse and I'm breathing. That exceeds all admission requirements. This is the bottom of the barrel. If I can't make it here, I can't make it anywhere." He mumbled something about a smart-ass and said, "Good luck. You're going to need it."

I did fine at MIT. Like the band Timbuk 3 said, *"I loved my classes. I had a crazy teacher who wore dark glasses. And things were going great. But they're only getting better. I was doing all right. Getting good grades. My future looked bright. I had to wear shades."* With 44 credits from the Milwaukee Institute of Technology, I transferred to Marquette University.

Two years later, I entered Marquette University Law School. I hated every minute of it. It was "learn by intimidation." Remember the movie *Paper Chase*? John Houseman played the imperious, sarcastic Professor Kingsley and Timothy Bottoms played the scared-to-death first year law student, James Hart. The classic opening scene accurately portrayed life at law school:

"Mister Hart, would you recite the facts of Hawkins versus McGee? I do have your name right? You are Mr. Hart? You're not speaking loud enough, Mister Hart. Mister HART. You're still not speaking loud enough. Will you STAND? Now that you're on your feet Mr. Hart, maybe the class will be able to understand you. YOU ARE ON YOUR FEET?"

"Yes I'm on my feet."

"Loudly MISTER HART. Fill the room with your intelligence. Now will you give us the facts of the case?"

"I haven't read the case."

"Class assignments for the first day are posted on the bulletin boards in Langdale and Austin Hall. You MUST have known that?"

"No."

"You assumed that the first class would be a LECTURE — an INTRODUCTION to the course?"

"Yes, sir."

"NEVER ASSUME ANYTHING IN MY CLASSROOM, Mister Hart."

Following more of the same, Mr. Hart ended his mortification by running out of the classroom and into the men's room where he threw up. I ended mine by graduating the year *Paper Chase* was released.

I practiced law for 17 years before handling my first Lemon Law case. In 1990, I received a call from a Chrysler employee. Ironically, he was having trouble with his new Chrysler-manufactured $25,000 Dodge conversion van. The transmission leaked and slipped. Chrysler couldn't fix it. They tried five times. To make matters worse, the van had sat in the shop for over 30 days.

My caller explained how he had asked Chrysler for a refund, but was turned down. He was told the van didn't qualify for a buyback under Wisconsin's Lemon Law. Chrysler assured him, however, that they would continue to make repairs under the warranty. I didn't know much about the Lemon Law, but something didn't seem right. Why didn't Chrysler just buy back the van?

I didn't want to tell my caller that he would be my first "lemon." Lawyers hate to admit ignorance. We have a knack for not letting on that we don't know what we're talking about. In law school, it's called "thinking on your feet." In real life it's called bullshitting. It is nothing to be proud of, but it is a characteristic of the profession. So, following in the tradition of all great legal minds, I asked my caller if I could get back to him in a day or two. There was something I wanted to check — **The Law**.

The next day I read the Lemon Law, went to the courthouse, got copies of every Lemon Law case filed in Wisconsin. We had a case. The Dodge van looked enough like a lemon to qualify for a buyback. I called my client with the good news. "You've got a case. What do you want, refund or replacement?"

Two months later, my client found himself in the unique position of biting the hand that fed him. Chrysler paid him to work and he sued them for damages. Could this be the American dream? Not according to Chrysler. Let me paraphrase their letter:

Your client should be eternally grateful for his job, do nothing to jeopardize it and get down on his knees every day and kiss the feet of Lee Iacocca for saving Chrysler from bankruptcy.

I'm not particularly fond of Lee Iacocca, and Chrysler should have bought this van back a long time ago. So I responded:

Don't EVER threaten my client or try to intimidate him because he works for Chrysler. The Lemon Law doesn't discriminate based on employment. And, you better not either. If you do, Lemon Law will be the least of your worries.

Employment status never came up again.

We bickered back and forth with Chrysler and finally settled before trial. Chrysler bought back the van for $45,733 plus attorney fees. Wisconsin is the only state that allows consumers to collect up to double damages if the manufacturer does not provide a refund or replacement within 30 days of the consumer's demand. In any other state, my client would have only been entitled to the $25,000 he paid for the van. Wisconsin gives the "little guy" leverage.

And, being the loyal Chrysler employee that he was, my client went out and bought a bigger, better Dodge van with more options. Unfortunately, his luck didn't change. The new van went up in flames in Memphis, Tennessee. Another lemon. Another buyback.

Over the next 13 years, I grew to love the Lemon Law.

What Took So Long?

Behold the warranty... the bold
print giveth and the fine print
taketh away.

— Anonymous

In 1908, the Ford Motor Company produced the first Model T. In 1982, Connecticut enacted the first Lemon Law. What took so long?

The American automobile industry began in 1896 when the Duryea Motor Wagon Company of Springfield, Massachusetts, produced 13 cars of the same design. Based on hearsay — and only hearsay — six of those cars were defective. Over the next 100 plus years, not much would change.

The bumper-to-bumper warranty, as we know it today, started out as a 60-day guarantee. However, in order to obtain the benefits of the guarantee, the owner had to deliver the car back to the Detroit factory or send the defective parts by mail, postage paid. Either way, enforcement was difficult, to say the least. It could take weeks to drive from Colorado to Detroit in 1911, even longer without second gear. For 34 years, the consumer was saddled with the 60-day guarantee until finally, the real **BREAKTHROUGH**.

In 1930, no doubt recognizing its obligation to the American car-buying public and the need for extended consumer protection, Detroit introduced the *incredible* 90 day/4,000 mile warranty, and you could take your car to the nearest dealer for repairs. At last, the auto buyer was given peace of mind. Car trouble days were over. Right.

By the 1950s, irate motor vehicle owners sounded identical to irate lemon owners of today.

"Detroit isn't living up to its warranties."
"The cars aren't safe. They're noisy, poorly designed."
"The dealers can't fix my concerns, even after
repeated repair attempts."

During this period, the American people wrote more letters to Congress and the Federal Trade Commission complaining about cars than about any other topic since the establishment of the FTC in 1914. Diana Shore might be singing, *"See the USA in your Chevrolet,"* but Americans were pissed! Their cars were defective and nobody cared.

Given the public outcry, presidents had to get involved. JFK sent the first Presidential Message on Consumer Affairs to Congress on March 15, 1962. President Johnson followed, demanding that warranties "… say what they mean and mean what they say." Milhous "I am not a crook" Nixon, recognized the real crooks. He established a powerful task force consisting of his Special Assistant for Consumer Affairs, representatives from the Departments of Commerce, Justice and Labor and the FTC to investigate the need for warranty legislation.

On March 1, 1971, in a message to Congress, Nixon proposed a Fair Warranty Disclosure Act, prohibiting the use of DECEPTIVE WARRANTIES. But, Detroit is a tough beast to bring down, even for presidents. Detroit is also devious.

In 1963, Chrysler had started a warranty revolution. Unfortunately it was all about sales, not repairs. The company announced an unprecedented 5 year/50,000 mile "powertrain warranty" covering all new Chrysler Corporation cars. For the first time, an automobile warranty was used as the primary sales tool. Why talk about defective cars that aren't selling when we can talk about how many years we will be willing to fix them? America took the bait… and the hook… and the sinker.

Chrysler sales skyrocketed 40 percent (as did Hyundai's in 2001 when the same technique brazenly claimed "America's Best Warranty" — 10 year/100,000 mile). A new era in consumerism began. GM, Ford and American Motors quickly followed suit.

By 1967, each of the "big four" offered virtually the identical warranty — 2 year/24,000 mile basic coverage and 5 year/50,000 mile powertrain coverage. Massive amounts of Madison Avenue money was poured into convincing the American car buyer that Detroit was finally ready, willing and eager to stand behind its product. The advertising paid off. New car sales increased dramatically for all of Motown and profits rolled. But NOTHING had really changed. In fact, things were going to get worse for the American car buyer.

Even though the new warranties were longer and appeared to give more protection, they heavily favored Detroit and were just as confusing and deceptive as the earlier 90-day warranties. Due to their obscure legal jargon, only corporate lawyers trained in deception were able to decipher their true hidden meaning. Mere human beings were left in the dark. In many instances, these warranties were actually used to take away consumer rights and remedies provided by other laws.

For example, the Uniform Commercial Code contains consumer protection laws enacted between 1954 and 1968 by every state except Louisiana. Later, between 1974 and 1988, Louisiana did enact parts of the code but not those relating to consumer protection. Mardi Gras apparently takes a toll on state legislators. I never buy anything in Louisiana. But I digress.

Under the UCC, every consumer who purchases goods (including a car) from a merchant (including a car dealer) receives certain implied warranties. One such warranty is the "implied warranty of merchantability." This guarantees that goods sold "are fit for the ordinary purposes for which they are used." If the goods turn out not to be "fit for the ordinary purposes" and are not repaired or replaced, the consumer has a legal claim for breach of the implied warranty.

The auto industry's written warranties, however, success-fully knocked out the UCC safeguards by incorporating specific disclaimer language:

> This warranty is expressly in lieu of all other war-ranties, express or implied, and all other obligations or liabilities.

Meaning, consumers could not resort to the UCC for redress. All they had were the provisions of Detroit's own written warranty, and that warranty provided only for repair or replace-ment of defective parts. Nothing more.

There was no guarantee that a problem would ever be fixed. There was no limit on the number of chances a dealer had to correct a problem. A defective transmission, for example, could be presented 15 times for repair. If it wasn't fixed by then, the consumer's only option was to take it back for the 16th time or trade it in. When the warranty expired, the consumer was left with no protection whatsoever.

Under the old 90-day warranties, dealers didn't fix cars. Under the new warranties, they could take years not to fix them. Besides, car dealers were in short supply, not enough to go around. There were too many defects, too many consumers, too many cars. A 1968 auto industry survey and a 1970 FTC report found that the most frequent and significant complaints by new car buyers were "unsatisfactory warranty service" and "the absolute refusal of dealers to honor the express warranties." In other words, Detroit had given consumers two options: **Poor Service or No Service.** Take it or leave it!

Detroit has always been a cavalier bastard, even naming a small Chevrolet after itself in 1982. Well, 8.5 million cars were produced in the United States in 1971. Every one of them came with a virtually useless warranty. Detroit was selling shoddy mer-chandise and couldn't or wouldn't fix it. Consumer protection statutes were grossly inadequate or nonexistent. Lawsuits against these Giants were cost prohibitive and doomed to fail.

These corporations had the wealth and will to exhaust individual litigants. Some things never change! They also controlled vast amounts of technical expertise on the very mechanical aspects that would be challenged.

Consumers begged for help. Congress investigated. Government encouraged the auto industry to voluntarily make warranties meaningful. Detroit's response? **The Italian Salute!** Something had to be done.

That something came in 1975 when President Gerald Ford attempted to shake up automobile warranty law by signing a confusing consumer protection law sometimes loosely referred to as the "Federal Lemon Law."

The Magnuson-Moss Warranty Act

The 1975 Magnuson-Moss Warranty Act, "Mag-Moss," was enacted to combat manufacturers' arrogance and widespread warranty-related problems, ESPECIALLY in the auto industry. The act was not limited to motor vehicles. It applied to all consumer products — televisions, refrigerators, sewing machines — anything covered by a written warranty. A 1969 government Task Force on Appliance Warranties and Service had found that manufacturer abuse was not limited to the auto industry. Purchasers of major appliances experienced the same warranty enforcement dilemmas as new car buyers. Whether you bought a Chevy or a stove, the treatment was the same. Corporate America's attitude sucked!

Mag-Moss was based on the premise that suppliers of goods vigorously used written warranties as advertising and merchandising come-ons. But if consumers were being sold goods based on warranty coverage, that coverage would have to mean something. It would also help immensely if consumers understood what the warranties said.

The starting point was simple. Mag-Moss recognized that the typical Detroit warranty was unclear, deceptive, unintelligible and written in print size that required high-powered magnification. Under Mag-Moss, manufacturers were ordered to clean up their act. From now on, warranties would have to be written in plain English with short, simple, straightforward sentences. Information had to be "fully and conspicuously" disclosed in "readily understood language." Print size had to be large enough to read, a truly unique concept. The day of "the small print" was over... allegedly.

Next, Mag-Moss stopped manufacturers from using their own written warranties to avoid liability. Detroit was no longer allowed to disclaim the implied warranties of the Uniform Commercial Code. They could, however, limit the duration of the implied warranties to the duration of their own written warranties.

For example, if General Motors provides a 3 year/36,000 mile written warranty on a new Silverado, they can limit the implied warranties of the Uniform Commercial Code to the same 3 year/36,000 miles. They must notify auto buyers in writing of such limitations. Mind you, the manufacturer is not REQUIRED to limit our rights. They are only given the ABILITY to limit our rights. Detroit could choose to do nothing, and new car buyers would retain the unlimited protection of the Uniform Commercial Code. But Detroit NEVER gives anything it doesn't have to give.

Today, virtually every manufacturer's New Vehicle Limited Warranty limits the duration of our rights under the Uniform Commercial Code. Just check out your own warranty booklet for the written notification.

Another important provision of Magnuson-Moss limited the number of chances a manufacturer and dealer had to repair warranty problems. No longer would you have to take your car in 16 times for transmission work. The act required that defects, malfunctions, and failures to conform with the warranty be repaired within a reasonable time without charge. If they were not so repaired, the consumer would have a claim and could sue for damages. Unfortunately, reasonable time was not defined. Still, any limitation was an improvement over pre-existing law that placed no limit on the number of repair attempts.

Twenty-five years of case law development — court rulings on issues that are not spelled out clearly in the statutes — have interpreted reasonable time in this instance to mean three or four visits to the repair shop for the same problem. If the dealer doesn't fix the problem by the third or fourth try, the consumer has a Mag-Moss claim.

The most significant provision of the Magnuson-Moss Warranty Act dealt with attorney fees. For the first time, consumers could sue Detroit on a warranty issue and make Detroit pay damages **and** legal fees. The Uniform Commercial Code had no similar provision. Neither did any other consumer warranty law. This fee shifting provision gave the courts discretion to award legal fees to consumers in warranty cases. Without the award of attorney fees, the little guy simply could not afford to sue Detroit.

In addition, Mag-Moss said attorney fees were to be based on actual time spent on the case, not tied to a percentage of recovery or limited by the amount in controversy. In other words, this was not your typical "I get one third of the amount you get" type case.

Make no mistake about it; the legal profession loves receiving one third of your $1,000,000 or your $200,000 or your $50,000. **LAWYERS: WE LOVE ONE THIRD** should be the catch phrase of the American Bar Association. But try to find an attorney willing to take your defective transmission case on a one third contingency. Try to find a lawyer interested in suing General Motors over a $1,200 repair bill for one third of the amount recovered. You can't. In all fairness to my fellow members of the bar, IT CAN'T BE DONE.

And, in all fairness to consumers, why should they receive only two thirds of their damages in warranty cases or, for that matter, in personal injury cases? But that's another issue.

For the first time, because of attorney fees if nothing else, Detroit was forced to take its warranty obligations seriously. If a consumer sued and won, regardless of the amount in controversy, the manufacturer could be hit with a huge legal bill. It didn't matter how much the consumer recovered — $1,000, $3,000, $10,000 — Detroit could have to pay the attorney fees. A $2,000 recovery might include a $25,000 attorney fee award. This imminent threat of attorney fees forced settlement of some cases that otherwise would have gone unaddressed.

Even though Magnuson-Moss seemed like a giant step forward, the act had many flaws. The act didn't apply to leases. It didn't define a reasonable number of repair attempts or make attorney fees mandatory. Mag-Moss also created the "informal dispute settlement procedure" or "mechanism," which provided the foundation for the Kangaroo Courts of Arbitration that permeate today's Lemon Laws.

Congress, in its self-proclaimed infallible wisdom, incapable of error in matters of consumer protection, gave consumers the right to sue the manufacturer. This was good. Then, Congress spoke. This was bad.

Said the voice of Congress:

"Even though most of us are lawyers, we don't really like lawsuits. We favor resolving disputes out of court. And, even though we gave consumers the right to sue Detroit, we would prefer that they didn't. It's better for the average guy to quickly resolve his dispute out of court. This saves the consumer from a long, drawn-out courtroom battle.

*"In order to accomplish this goal, we want all manufacturers to set up **THEIR OWN** arbitration programs to deal with consumer warranty issues. This way, the same companies that*

have been screwing car buyers since 1896 can continue to screw them in arbitration, but now with the Congressional Seal of Approval."

Government is a very slow learner. Remember, the only reason we have a Magnuson-Moss Act in the first place is because Presidents, Governmental Bodies, Task Forces, Commissions, Councils, and Departments could not **ENCOURAGE OR PERSUADE** manufacturers to voluntarily stop sticking it to the American consumer. So, how does Congress respond? By allowing the auto industry to set up its own "courts" and requiring that consumers first resort to these programs before going to real courts of justice.

Although Mag-Moss attempted to include safeguards to protect the consumer from unfair and biased manufacturer influence, ultimately, it was not much different than letting corporate America police itself. If the Catholic Church can't police itself, how can Detroit?

The enthusiasm for Magnuson-Moss quickly died. The act failed miserably to alleviate new car buyer problems. Detroit fought car cases like wars and beat down the average Joe and Joe's average lawyer.

The auto companies exploited every loophole available to avoid giving refunds or replacements. For example, Mag-Moss provided that if a manufacturer issued a "FULL WARRANTY" with a product and the product turned out to be defective and not repaired within a reasonable time, the consumer had an absolute right to a refund or replacement. But if the manufacturer issued only a "LIMITED WARRANTY," the consumer was limited to damages — financial compensation — only. A refund was unlikely, a replacement out of the question.

You don't have to be Einstein to figure out what happened. Detroit stopped issuing full warranties. To this day, every new car in America comes with a limited warranty, thanks to Congress and Magnuson-Moss.

American Corporations
that have Failed at Policing Themselves

3M
Abbott Laboratories
Adelphia Communications
Advance PCS
Aether Systems
American Electric Power
Andrx
Arthur Anderson
Ask Jeeves Inc.
AstraZeneca
Aventis Pharmaceuticals
B Square
Bank One
Bayer
Bears Stearns
Boeing
Bristol-Myers Squibb
Broadway National Bank
Brown & Williamson
Caremark Rx
Cendant Corp.
Citigroup
Clarent
ConAgra Foods
Concur Technologies
Copper Mountain Networks
Credit Suisse First Boston
Critical Path
CUC International
Datek Online
Deloitte & Touche
Deutsche Bank Securites

Dial Corp.
drugstore.com
Duke Energy
Dynegy
E.piphany
eFunds Corp.
El Paso Corp.
Electronic Data Systems
EndoVascular Technologies
Enron
Ernst & Young
Expedia
Express Scripts
F5 Networks
Firestone
FleetBoston Financial
Fleming
Ford
Freddie Mac
GlaxoSmithKline
Global Crossing
Goldman Sachs
Greeting Cards of America
H & R Block
HealthSouth
Homestore
Household Finance
ImClone
Informix
InfoSpace
Internap
J. P. Morgan

Kimberly-Clark
LaBranche & Co.
Lehman Brothers
Levi Strauss
Liggett
Lorillard
Lucent
Marimba
Martha Stewart
McDonald's
Medco Health Solutions
Merrill Lynch
Metropolitan Life
Mirant
Montana Power
Morgan Stanley
mp3.com
Nextel Partners
Nike
Onyx Software
Pfizer
Phillip Morris
PricewaterhouseCoopers
Quest Communications
R.J. Reynolds Tobacco
Raytheon
Red Hat

Reliant Resources
Rent-A-Center
Rite Aid
Robertson Stephens
San Diego Gas & Electric
Sara Lee
Schering-Plough
Solomon Smith Barney
Southern California Gas
Symbol Technologies
Tenet Healthcare
theglobe.com
Thomas Weisel Partners
TiVo, Inc.
Tyco International
Tyson Foods
U.S. Bancorp Piper Jaffray
U.S. Technologies
UBS Warburg
United States Tobacco
VA Linux
Vivendi Universal
Wal-Mart
Williams Cos.
WorldCom
Xcel Energy
Xerox

Miss Cleo's Psychic Hotline,
the Archdiocese of Boston,
Cardinal Bernard Law, and
the Catholic Church.

Amendments to the act were proposed in 1979 to close the full versus limited warranty loophole. Under the amendments, all new car warranties would have to be full warranties. New car manufacturers would be required to satisfy the repair or replacement mandates of the Magnuson-Moss Act or stop offering written warranties. The proposals died in committee and were not reintroduced. The Beast is powerful.

After only a few short years, it became clear that Mag-Moss did little to improve the consumer's position. Again something had to be done. This time, that something occurred in 1982 when Connecticut became the first state to enact a LEMON LAW.

Note

Just one year after the first state Lemon Law was passed, Congress had another opportunity to correct its Magnuson-Moss blunder. The Automobile Consumer Protection Act of 1983 was introduced. This act was an attempt to create a uniform federal Lemon Law, very similar to the state Lemon Laws that exist today. Congress did not even pay lip service to this bill, which was completely and utterly disregarded, shelved at a time when consumers were crying out for protection.

A *Roper Report* issued that same year found that 66 percent of consumers surveyed desperately wanted Lemon Law protection even if it meant adding $100 to the price of a new car. However, Detroit did not want a uniform federal Lemon Law, and Detroit has a seat in Congress.

Like a Woman

They're treating me like I'm stupid, like I don't know anything.
They're treating me like an idiot, like I'm some kind of moron.
They're treating me like a woman.

Over and over my female clients complain, "I'm being
treated like a woman." My usual response is something to the
effect of, "This business really sucks. I know they took advantage
of you. You think it was because you are a woman and to some
extent that's true. But, if you sat on this side of the desk, you'd
know that the industry takes advantage of anyone and everyone
it can, woman or not."

Everyone is a target for a Detroit screwing — minorities,
the poor, uneducated, young, old, farmers, factory workers,
accountants, doctors and even lawyers if they can get away with
it. Caveat Emptor — Buyer Beware — more than ever, rules the
day.

See Joe. He'll Give You a Good Deal.

Nancy C. was a senior at the University of Wisconsin. She needed a car. A friend, or so she thought, referred her to Joe F., a salesman at a local Volkswagen dealership. Joe was good at his job. He sold her a 1996 VW Certified Used Passat with 63,000 miles for sticker price, $12,995. Nancy didn't get a discount. Like many young buyers, she didn't know she could negotiate, and Joe was a true salesman. Notwithstanding the referral, he treated her like a woman. And that's not the end of it.

Before buying the car, Nancy asked if she could take it for a drive.

"Of course," Joe responded. "This car's a dream. Let me grab the keys and we'll go for a spin."

Nancy was excited to get behind the wheel of her first nice car. She drove on city streets and the freeway. The car was perfect — power, handling, color, everything. She told Joe how much she liked it. (Never tell a salesman how much you like anything he is selling. It does nothing for your bargaining power.)

On the way back to the dealership, Nancy noticed something. The Anti-lock Brake System light was on. She asked Joe if there was a problem.

"No, that's not a problem," he quickly replied. "This car has anti-lock brakes. The light is supposed to be on. Don't worry about anything. You have VW certification. You're covered for 2 years/24,000 miles." Nancy bought the car.

Three weeks later, the ABS light was still on. Not a problem, according to Joe. However, now the headlights didn't work. That was a problem, a major problem. Nancy took the car in for warranty work. The dealer fixed the headlights. And the dealer fixed the ABS light. The ABS light was NOT supposed to be on. There was a short in the system. JOE HAD LIED! I know you find that hard to believe.

Over the next year, the Certified VW was an electrician's dream — engine light, ABS light, wiring harness, coolant light, brake lights, fuses, air bags, defroster, ignition, and instrument cluster — all defective. One service adviser told Nancy he watched fuses blow and spark as they were being replaced. Nancy called my office to see if there was anything she could do. We filed a claim against the dealer for the lies of Joe.

Most of my cases are the Lemon Law, Magnuson-Moss type warranty claims against auto manufacturers. My clients have car trouble. They take their car in for repairs. The problems aren't fixed within a reasonable time. We file suit. However, I have nothing against suing car dealerships for fraudulent mis-representation. In fact, I kind of enjoy it. There are consumer protection laws, but dealers are shrewd operators. They're usually harder to catch than Mario Andretti on the Autobahn. Not this time. Nancy settled for a total refund.

Sticker Plus

When the Chrysler PT Cruiser first came out in 1999, you couldn't find one. They were being sold faster than they could be produced. (Why, I don't know. Some riding mowers had more horse power.) Dealers were taking orders and asking thousands of dollars over sticker, perfectly legal.

Car dealers are not prohibited from charging more than the Manufacturer's Suggested Retail Price, and would like to do it more often. But today, the Cruiser is discounted like any other vehicle because the fad is over. KIAs have never sold for over sticker.

Adele J. called my office telling me that she was ripped off by a local KIA dealer. My initial thought was, so what else is new? Except that Adele wasn't calling because she bought a KIA. She was calling because they treated her like a woman.

In her words, "I'm a black woman. I didn't know anything about buying a car. The dealer didn't treat me with respect. They took advantage of me."

I was curious to find out what happened. Adele sounded sincere and I could tell that she felt hurt, by the tone of her voice.

Adele had been looking for her first new car. The KIA Spectra at $13,500 seemed to fit her budget. She didn't realize that $13,500 was only the Manufacturer's Suggested Retail Price and this new car buyer, like Nancy, was simply unaware of the need to negotiate. She just assumed car shopping was like shopping at Sears. The price on the washing machine was the price you paid.

So, I thought, okay. They took you for sticker. I don't like it, but it happens every day. There's nothing we can do about it. Then, Adele gave me her real gripe.

She didn't pay sticker. She paid $1,000 OVER sticker — $14,500 — without knowing it. This is the first KIA I've heard of going for a premium. There is no KIA shortage. There is no KIA demand problem. Spectras and Rios are stacked up in Seoul, South Korea, just waiting for the next ship to America. Adele was flimflammed. She was scammed. The dealer categorized her as a sucker and treated her like a woman. Here's how they did it:

The motor vehicle purchase contract is a complicated document, especially for someone looking at it for the first time. There are many blank spaces to be filled in with dollar amounts at the time of purchase.

Retail Price, MSRP, Cash Price, Trade-in Allowance, State Tax, County Tax, Stadium Tax (I still don't understand why I pay for the Milwaukee Brewers' Stadium. They are a private enterprise. They lose most of their games and they don't pay for my house.) Registration, Title, Down Payment, Balance Due, Additional Cash Due, Due on Delivery, Balance to Finance, and the list goes on. Once numbers appear in these spaces, the contract becomes even more confusing.

In Adele's case, $13,500 was always the agreed sales price. The salesman wrote that price in the appropriate space. When he showed Adele the contract, she saw $13,500 as the sales price.

What she didn't see was that the salesman had also written $1,000 in a space called Dealer Markup Added. Because of the location of the Dealer Markup space, about two inches above the sales price space, it would have been very easy for the salesman to cover the $1,000 figure with his hand or finger while Adele signed the contract. Once signed, the contract was folded and stuffed into an envelope. Adele's daughter caught the $1,000 markup when she looked over the contract at home.

You might ask why Adele didn't just return the car. She has three days, to reconsider a contract, doesn't she? **WRONG!** You don't have three minutes to get out of an automobile purchase contract, unless it was signed in a tent off the premises.

The Three Day Right of Cancellation is widely misunderstood. In general, it only applies to sales that occur AWAY from a place of business, not to sales that occur at a place of business. For example, if you buy that Kirby vacuum cleaner of your dreams from a door-to-door peddler, or custom aluminum siding at the Mendocino County Fair, you have three days to rethink your decision and back out of the contract. Not so if you VISIT your friendly Ford store and sign on the dotted line.

Wish I could say that we sued the dealer and recovered $25,000 for Adele. We didn't. I turned down the case. I knew Adele was scammed. I knew she got screwed, but we couldn't prove it. Everything was in writing. She signed the contract. She received a copy. I hated what had happened, but there was nothing we could do. As an old attorney friend of mine once said, "It looks like we're out of the boat and into the water on this one."

Crazy Jim and the Wood Block

Crazy Jim sold cars. Crazy Jim ran for governor. Crazy Jim sponsored a Demolition Derby. And on May 31, 2001, Crazy Jim treated Marisa C. like a very special woman.

Marisa paid $5,500 for a 1993 Chevy pickup truck with 134,000 miles. She didn't expect perfection. She didn't expect new. She also didn't expect to find a wood block jammed between the frame and body of her truck in order to keep it from wobbling. Even for the auto industry, this was egregious conduct. The lack of moral accountability in this business never ceases to amaze me.

Six weeks after purchasing the pickup, Marisa failed the state emissions test for the second time. She contacted a car care center for advice and found she'd be able to pass emissions with a new catalytic converter and a tune-up. However, she had far more serious trouble on her hands.

The truck had major frame damage. The cab leaned to one side and swiveled. A wood block about the size of a 2" x 4" had been shoved between the frame and body to offset a frame imbalance. This truck was not safe to drive. It shouldn't be on the road. Marisa was told to take it back to Crazy Jim.

Crazy told Marisa that there wasn't any problem. The wood block was supposed to be there. It was part of a "lift up kit" that had been installed to raise the truck. Marisa called Crazy "crazy" and drove to a nearby Chevy dealer for another opinion. Braeger Chevrolet in Milwaukee confirmed the problem. Using a 2" x 4" to shim a frame, unless you're building a house, is not acceptable. The truck was unsafe. Marisa was told not to drive it. Braeger even gave her a letter to that effect. She went back to Crazy Jim's.

Nothing had changed. Crazy stuck to his story. The truth to a liar is like daylight to a vampire. The wood block was part of the "lift up kit." It belonged in the frame. Braeger Chevrolet and the car care center technician didn't know what they were talking about. THEY were crazy! Crazy suggested that Marisa sell the vehicle if she wasn't happy. Marisa told Crazy that he sold her a "piece of shit that couldn't be driven on the road." She asked for a refund. Crazy replied, "Unfortunately, we can't give you your money back, young lady. We don't do that."

We nailed Crazy. We got Marisa's money back and Crazy paid our attorney fees. We won, but this is just one case.

What about all the other "young ladies" out there who spend hard-earned money on crap used cars, who are lied to, intimidated? And, like I said, it's not just women.

Not Just Women

Chris was a sophomore at Florida State University. His 2002 Camaro had bad brakes. University Chevrolet of Tallahassee machined the front rotors, under warranty, at 11,000 and 19,000 miles, but the pulsation continued. Chris drove home to Milwaukee in late summer. The brakes were worse than ever; they needed to be fixed. What better place to take the car than the selling dealer. After all, this is the same dealership that sent out those thank-you letters promising "100% Satisfaction."

The Camaro limped to the original dealership in Milwaukee and to a service consultant. There was one hitch. "Rotors are not covered under warranty," the consultant explained. "You'll have to pay for brake work."

Chris passed Freshman English. He had basic reading skills. He read the 2002 Camaro Warranty. Brake rotors WERE covered under warranty for 3 years/36,000 miles. Only pads and linings were excluded. Knowing I love nothing more than talking about car problems, Chris called my office to find out whether he had to pay for brake work. My first thought was, if Chris were female he'd be saying, "They're treating me like a woman."

I know Chevrolet's warranty like the back of my hand. Rotors are definitely covered. The dealer was wrong. Why were they giving this kid the runaround? They sold him the car. They sent him those letters. I phoned the dealer and questioned the service consultant about the rotors. He told me, "Rotors are not covered. This is a maintenance item. GM will only cover them up to 12,000 miles." After a brief discussion with this bullheaded bastard who apparently did not pass Freshman English, I read him my version of the Riot Act.

"Do you KNOW the difference between pads and rotors? Have you ever READ a warranty? What does 'bumper-to-bumper' MEAN? Can you define PUNITIVE DAMAGES? Are you aware that your dealership AND General Motors can be SUED for willfully refusing to perform warranty repairs?"

I was advised to calm down.

"We can handle this in a professional manner," he said. "There is no need to raise your voice."

But no matter how professional we got, the rotors still weren't covered. The consultant claimed that the service manager, who was on vacation, was the only person who could authorize the repair. In the meantime, he suggested I call GM and get it straight from the "horse's mouth," or wherever. He asked if I needed the phone number.

"I've sued General Motors 350 times. I don't need their stinking number and I don't care what they have to say about anything! This car is in YOUR shop. YOU are the authorized dealer. YOU sold it. YOU fix it. It's unsafe. And if you WON'T fix it, make sure you give me a repair order stating your dealership REFUSES to repair the car under warranty."

He replied calmly, "I can't write that down, sir. I'm not refusing to fix it, I just don't have authority."

I yelled back, "You DO have authority. YOU'RE the authorized dealer. If you don't have authority, NOBODY does. We don't have to drive to Michigan for warranty work. We don't have to FedEx the brakes to Detroit. FIX THE CAR."

My phone receiver then contacted the cradle with a resonance that echoed through the office.

The next day's news from the consultant was alarming. The car shouldn't be driven. The brakes were bad. They were grinding and pulsating. Still, the dealership wouldn't do the repair. The consultant wanted to keep the car six more days until his service manager returned from vacation. This repair was "way beyond my jurisdiction."

I suggested he keep the Camaro for 30 days, eliminating the need for a "brake job" altogether. GM could then simply give my client a new car based on the "30 days out of service" provision found in most states' Lemon Laws. That way, everybody wins: Chris gets a new car, the consultant's interpretation of the warranty is followed, and General Motors saves $300 on rotors. No deal.

Chris picked up his Camaro and drove it across town to another dealer. The rotors were quickly replaced by a dealer who understood the warranty and the young Bobby Bowden fan got back to Tallahassee in time to see Florida State beat Iowa State. Thanks to the "impeccable service" of the original Chevrolet dealership, Chris now had four repair orders documenting defective brakes, should the thought of a Lemon Law suit ever cross his collegiate mind. And it may. Chris is my son.

I Am Woman

I too have been treated like a woman. My first time was by a Cadillac dealer. About three years ago, I received a special invitation in the mail. It wasn't sent to just anyone. I was a preferred customer. I had attained preferred status by dropping my business card in the free-lunch-drawing fishbowl when I was at the dealership returning a client's lemon. My neighbor Ralph wasn't a preferred customer. He didn't get an invitation. He didn't drop his card in the fishbowl. If Ralph wanted a Cadillac, he'd have to pay top buck. Who knows, this dealer might not even sell to Ralph. I felt privileged to be in this elite group of humanity.

The invitation told me that 50 new Cadillacs were being sold at incredible savings. All would be at, or below, invoice. Some were $10,000 below invoice. Others were $15,000 off MSRP. All 50 would be at the dealership, clearly designated and priced. There would be no need to negotiate. The sale would last three days. I was instructed to bring the invitation AND identification with me. Ralph could not sneak in with my letter.

I arrived at the dealership with driver's license and invite in hand. A friendly salesman approached me with a "No one will beat my deal" handshake. I told him I was a preferred customer and would like to see some of the specials. He said, "I've got a red Eldorado with your name on it, loaded, $15,000 below sticker."

Fifteen grand off of an Eldorado would be a great deal. They list for about $40, 000. If I could buy an Eldorado for 25 Gs, I'd be happy. We walked over for a closer look.

This Eldorado didn't list at $40,000. The sticker was $68,000. It had every Cadillac option and $25,000 of after-market accessories — those options installed after the vehicle leaves the factory. The convertible wasn't even factory. Originally a sedan, the top had been cut off at some "chop shop."

The tires weren't factory issue either or the rims, stereo, alarm, radar detector and who knew what else. This was a $53,000 circus-mobile, an after-market nightmare. I asked to see some traditional Cadillacs. My salesman said he'd be right back.

He returned with bad news. He couldn't locate any other Cadillacs that were part of the promotion. Apparently they were all sold, but I was assured that a great deal could be worked out on any car I liked.

That wasn't good enough. I specifically came to see 50 cars priced at incredible savings. So far, I had seen one Frankensteined Eldorado. I called the salesman a liar to his face. He got his manager. I called the manager a liar to HIS face. He asked me to leave. I asked him to show me 49 purchase contracts for the 49 cars that were sold during the preferred customer promotion.

Next came the general manager. I called him a liar to his face. He told me, "If you don't leave, I'm going to call the cops."

I said, "I'll wait right here until they come. Then we'll all talk about it." About ten minutes later the owner approached.

"Vince," he said, "why are you breaking my balls?" Well, considering the language, this was the first time today I wasn't being treated like a woman.

"We're just trying to make a living," he told me. "We're not trying to pull anything.

"If you want a car, pick one out. You can have it at cost. You can even take the 3 percent dealer holdback. I won't make a penny on you. Just tell me what you want."

I said, "I want all the bullshit to stop. I don't want to be told that I'm a select customer, told that I need a special invitation to spend $45,000, told that no one else can buy at these prices. You and I both know if that guy across the street leaving McDonalds with his Big Mac came over here with 50,000 bucks, you'd get down on your knees and kiss his ass to make a deal. I don't want to be treated like an idiot, like I'm stupid. I don't want to be treated like a woman." I didn't get a car.

My second time was at the hands of a Lincoln dealer, where I became part of the "lost leader" scam. My wife, Connie, was in the market for a new car. She liked the Lincoln LS because of its style and drivability. I liked it because I hate Ford. The LS was a new model. First-year models are usually more problematic. We'd have a shot at another lemon. I have no problem with Detroit covering my transportation cost.

I saw an ad in the Saturday morning paper for a base model Lincoln LS at an exceptional price — around $25,000. I'm well aware of the cliché, "If it sounds too good to be true, it probably is." I'm also aware of the penalties for false advertising. I grabbed a Diet Coke and headed to the showroom. Connie doesn't always enjoy going car shopping with me. She says it usually ends up adversarial. I just don't know where she gets that idea.

Everyone was so happy at the dealership. "How can we help you? What can we do for you? Can we offer you coffee or popcorn?" My sales executive asked if I had anything in mind. I explained that I had seen the ad for the LS and was interested. He said the new Lincoln was one of the hottest cars on the market. "We're having trouble keeping them on the lot."

He showed me three. All were priced well into the 30s. I asked to see the $25,000 base model that was advertised. Again, bad luck. Just like at the Cadillac dealership, that particular LS had been sold. I missed out. Somebody got there before me, but there was no need to worry. My exec told me I wouldn't want the base model. The 6-cylinder engine was too small. I'd be much happier with a V-8.

I said, "I don't want a V-8. I don't want to pay $35,000. I want the $25,000 Lincoln advertised in the paper."

I talked to three managers. The general manager finally showed me actual sales contracts. In eight months, the dealer had sold two base model Lincolns. The most recent sale had been four months earlier. No one beat me to the dealership that morning. They had no intention of selling anybody a $25,000 Lincoln. This was truly a "lost leader" — a product that does not exist being advertised at a very low price. It's akin to a "bait and switch" scam where a cheap, stripped down product is adver- tised for an incredibly low price. When you go to buy it, you are persuaded that the cheap model isn't for you. You are then switched into the more expensive product. In the lost leader scam, you can't even find the product.

The general manager told me they kept one base model LS at their dealership in Madison. They would sell it, but only if forced to do so. "It's a lost leader," he said.

I was shocked. Someone had finally admitted the truth. This Lincoln Mercury dealer was openly and flagrantly treating everybody like a woman. And nobody seemed to care. Again I didn't get a car.

Afterthought

The dealers know the law. The dealers know when they lie. The widespread misrepresentation in the car industry will only be stopped when more private attorneys take these cases. Writing letters to the Better Business Bureau is simply not going to do it.

Those personal injury lawyers on every street corner in America handing out cards, begging for one third of your settlement, should start representing consumers who get taken at the car lot, not just hit from behind.

The Runaround

Never listen when they tell you
that Man and the animals have a
common interest, that the prosperity
of the one is the prosperity of the
others. It is all lies.

— George Orwell
Animal Farm

In December 2002, Walter W. took his first step into the ever circling world of the automotive runaround.

Walter was a young chiropractor. He was married with two small children. He put $8,000 down on a Lincoln LS and signed a three-year lease. One year after delivery, the Lincoln began to stink. It stunk so bad that his family wouldn't ride in it and the dealer couldn't fix it.

Walter called the Lincoln Customer Relations Center for help. He spoke with Deja. Deja told him to pay off the lease and buy a new car. He called back and spoke with Chester. Chester said nothing could be done. Walter asked for Chester's supervisor. He was given to Josie. Josie said, "Go back to your dealer." Walter went back to his dealer and saw Max. Max said, "Scott will call you." But Scott never called.

Walter called the Center again. He talked to Charley. Charley said, "Stick with your dealer." Walter said, "I want Ford to take back the LS." Charley said, "Ford doesn't buy cars back.

The dealer does." Walter called the dealer and spoke to sales manager Storniolo. Storniolo said, "We don't buy cars. Customer Relations doesn't know what they're talking about. They answer phones. You can tell 'em I said that."

Walter called Customer Relations again. He talked with Morgan. Walter told Morgan what Storniolo said. Morgan called Storniolo and then called Walter and told him to call Red Carpet Leasing for "early termination." Walter called Red Carpet. He talked to Ben. They were disconnected. He called back. He talked to Tracy. They were disconnected. He called back. He talked to Kimberly. Kimberly told Walter that his best bet would be to trade in the car.

Walter called my office and said, "I'm getting the runaround." We filed a lawsuit. That's one way to stop the runaround. Walter returned his stinking LS and received $12,000 plus attorney fees.

The last thing Detroit wants to do is buy back cars. There's no profit in buybacks — no gains, only losses. The auto industry hates the Lemon Laws. Have no doubts about this. If they could lobby them out of existence they would. In fact, Detroit has done a pretty good job of rendering Lemon Laws meaningless in many states. But in the majority of states where Lemon Laws are effective, the industry resorts to the runaround in order to avoid the buyback.

Detroit has made an art form out of delay and deception when dealing with owners of problematic vehicles. Pass the buck, wear the consumer down, knock the consumer out — it's all part of the game. And it all starts with the dealer.

The Dealer Runaround

The authorized dealer is the consumer's link to Detroit. Nowhere in the warranty book am I told I can take my Mustang directly to Ford World Headquarters in Dearborn, Michigan, for repairs. If I have a problem, I am instructed to contact an author-ized dealer, preferably the selling dealer. GM's warranty booklet assures me that my Chevrolet dealer wants me "completely sat-isfied." Ford tells me that my dealer has made a "commitment" to me. Even KIA says my dealer will "take care" of me.

Chrysler doesn't make any such promises. I read my wife's 300M warranty booklet cover to cover and found nothing similar. Maybe Chrysler dealers just don't care.

Going to your selling dealer to talk about a lemon is like going to the Bayou Knights of the Ku Klux Klan to talk about inte-gration. They don't want to hear about it, talk about it or even acknowledge its existence. **LEMON** is a bad, bad word around a dealership. No matter what the warranty booklet tells you, your friendly dealer isn't going to be very friendly when you drop by and say, "My car is a lemon."

Those words won't bring the general manager forward with a smile and a handshake. He isn't going to say, "Thank you for making us aware of your concerns. As you know, your satis-faction is our number one goal. If I could just ask you to have a seat in our customer lounge, I'll process your refund request immediately. Bookkeeping should have a check in about 15 minutes. In the meantime, please help yourself to complimen-tary donuts and coffee. As always, it has been a pleasure working with you and your family. I hope this unfortunate incident will not discourage you from visiting our dealership in the future."

Quite the contrary. Your dealer is going to do everything in his power to "nip it in the bud," as Barney Fife would say, to stop the craziness before it begins, to encourage you, ONE WAY OR ANOTHER, not to seek Lemon Law relief. Once Lemon Law has been threatened, your dealer will lose what little credibility he ever had and go on a lying jag.

Here are some examples of what dealers have said to my clients once the "**L Word**" was spoken:

- If you lemon this, we won't work on it.
- Ford is not in the business of buying back their vehicles.
- As long as we keep trying to fix it, you can't file a Lemon Law claim.
- Well, if you're going to do that (Lemon Law), we're all done talking.
- You don't have a lemon. I'll work a deal on a trade.
- These companies are too big to fight. You can't win.
- I'm supposed to do whatever I can to prevent you from getting a new vehicle. (This statement came from a Chrysler dealer. It may explain why I couldn't find any dealer promise or commitment in my wife's 300M warranty booklet. At least this guy was honest. You almost feel like buying a car from him.)

Customer Assistance Runaround

Consumers are often told to call Customer Assistance when they have a car problem. Welcome to another runaround. The people you talk to have little or no authority, have been trained to deny and may not even be employees of the industry. Consider General Motors.

On January 30, 2003, I called GMC Customer Assistance — 1-800-GMC-8782. I spoke with Lonnie Reynolds. I asked Lonnie if he was an employee of General Motors. He refused to answer that question. I asked Lonnie what city he was in. He wouldn't tell me. I asked Lonnie if GM signed his paycheck. He wouldn't tell me that either. Lonnie was a very secretive CA representative. He told me to call the GM Business Resource Center at 1-800-231-1841 for the information I was seeking. I thanked Lonnie for his assistance — he was truly a helpful individual in his own way — and called the BRC.

I spoke with Nancy Klotz. Ms. Klotz told me that Customer Assistance was in partnership with General Motors. I asked if that meant Customer Assistance personnel were employees of General Motors. Again, I was told it was a partnership. It seemed like a straightforward question to me. Are customer assistance personnel employees of GM? Ms. Klotz wouldn't give me a yes or no answer. I asked to speak with her supervisor.

I was getting the runaround just trying to find out the employment status of customer assistance personnel. I had heard that GM customer assistance people weren't employees of General Motors. That seemed puzzling. Who are these people? What authority do they have? Why am I calling them? If I'm having problems with my Chevy Malibu, I want to talk to Chevrolet. I want Chevy to "Be There," just like in their ads.

Marcus came to the phone. He refused to give me his last name. He was probably concerned it would appear in print some day. Why would he think that? People are just so skeptical nowadays. Marcus said GM contracts the people working the call centers. In other words, they are not GM employees. They work for independent firms hired by General Motors.

This is kind of like the call I get every year from someone claiming to be with the Waukesha County Sheriff's Department seeking my support for the annual Safe Halloween Party. I donated one time — 16 years ago — and will never be taken off the sucker list. The people who call me each year aren't with the Sheriff's Department. They're not with any law enforcement agency. They just pretend to be. The people who call me each year are independent telemarketers from New Jersey who get 40 percent of whatever I contribute.

I hassle them every time they call. I tell them to take me off the list. I tell them I will never give a dime to any sheriff's organization for any reason because of this continuing scam. I tell them I hate Halloween, kids don't need a party, and I donate to the Rescue Mission. Then I hang up. The following July I get another call.

Personally, I would never call Customer Assistance for assistance.

Their job is to get the monkey off Detroit's back any which way they can. They lie, cheat, deny, intimidate, procrastinate, discourage, mislead, confuse, delay, and once in a while — if really pushed — throw an extended warranty or owner appreciation certificate your way. Vanna White gives away cars. Customer Assistance doesn't.

Here are some examples of what my clients have been told by Customer Assistance:

- I'm not going to buy back your car.
- You don't have to get an attorney. We know what to do.
- All we are going to do is keep fixing it.
- We are not going to do anything because it's still under warranty.
- Go ahead, sue us.
- Your car doesn't qualify under the Lemon Law.
- Trucks aren't covered by the Lemon Law.
- Wisconsin doesn't HAVE a Lemon Law.
- Vince Megna is just working for himself. He doesn't have his client's interest in mind. He has a reputation at our office. (This statement was made by a GM customer service rep who offered my client four new tires, instead of a new car, to settle his case.)

The TSB Runaround

Every couple of weeks I get a call from an irate Chevy truck owner who tells me, "My engine knocks and the dealer just gave me some kind of bulletin that says nothing's wrong, don't worry about it. What can I do?"

I know exactly what my caller is talking about. GM has recognized a cold start engine knock affecting 1999–2002

Chevrolet and GMC pickups. This condition has been around for years and GM can't fix it. So, they did the next best thing. They issued a Technical Service Bulletin.

TSBs provide dealership personnel with diagnostic and corrective information on recurring problems or conditions in certain vehicle models. The one related to this man's truck, TSB 01-06-01-028, stated that General Motors Powertrain Engineering confirmed that the engine knocking on cold starts "is not detrimental to the performance, reliability, or durability of the engine."

Whew. This has to be a relief to anyone who's just put out $36,000 for one of the "World's Most Powerful Pickups." If a company statement says it's not a problem, who are we to question? After all, when was the last time a corporate entity lied to us? One would have to go back hours, maybe even days.

I don't know if the condition described in that bulletin presents a problem or not, but it looks, smells and acts like a runaround. When Detroit issues a TSB saying nothing is WRONG, it usually means something IS wrong. If NOTHING were wrong, they wouldn't have to put out the TSB. I do know that if I were looking for a new truck and the engine knocked, I wouldn't buy it. Plain and simple. Engines aren't supposed to knock. That's why they don't tell us about the knock until after the purchase. They don't have the moral fortitude — or CORPORATE BALLS — to tell us before. They could lose a sale. We might buy a Dodge. Heaven forbid.

So, they follow the advice of the Steve Miller Band, and "*Take the Money and Run.*" Then, when the loyal customer returns to the dealer complaining about engine noise, he's given a TSB and told, "There's nothing to worry about. Keep making your payments."

I'd like to see TSB 01-06-01-028 plastered on the window of every new Chevy truck on the showroom floor. Consumers could then make informed decisions before spending their money instead of going into cardiac arrest when the dealer says, "We know. We can't fix it but it's not a problem."

Even I Get the Runaround

My first personal lawsuit against General Motors was over my 1997 White Diamond DeVille. It pulled. GM dealers worked on it many times, but it wouldn't go straight. Finally, while the lawsuit was pending, a service writer said he found the problem: the tires. I can still see him running his hands over the tread of the Michelins, shaking his head.

"The tires are bad. You can feel the cupping. You've got ply separation."

He even had me run MY hand over the front passenger tire to show me the problem.

"You're gonna have to replace 'em."

This is good. I'm in the middle of my lawsuit with General Motors and this guy confirms a defect. I'll make sure he is added to the witness list. Hey, wait a minute. My new witness wants ME to pay for the tires. He is trying to sell me tires.

I say, "My tires are covered under warranty."

He replies, "The only warranty you have is from the tire manufacturer. GM doesn't warrant tires. You can buy the tires here and send the receipt to Michelin for partial reimbursement."

I'm not this stupid. I mean, I did graduate from law school, albeit in the middle of my class, but I am not a half-wit. Yet, I must appear to be one. I pull out my warranty book. General Motors does cover tires. The exact wording:

> The tires supplied with your vehicle are covered against defects in material or workmanship under the bumper-to-bumper coverage.

I don't have to go to Michelin. I don't have to submit a receipt for partial reimbursement. If the tires are defective, GM, NOT THE TIRE MANUFACTURER, will replace them at no charge. I hand the booklet to the service writer. This is when I find out he can't read. He hands it back to me.

"General Motors doesn't warrant tires," he tells me. "You are going to have to contact Michelin."

I ask him, "Are my tires defective? Are they cupping? Are they separating? Did you read the warranty? Can you find your ass with both hands in the dark?" Again, my witness responds.

"Your General Motors Warranty doesn't cover tires. You'll have to take this up with Michelin."

No, I'm not going to Michelin. This is about Crest Cadillac. I announce, "I'm going to talk to your manager."

With these words, I suddenly flashed back to an incident in my law school days. Two musician friends of mine, Dick and Tony, were salesmen at one of Milwaukee's largest Chevrolet dealerships. I'd visit them from time to time to talk about music, why we were in Vietnam, and any other relevant issues of the day. On one of my visits, I learned what "talking to the manager" really meant.

I was sitting in Tony's office. Dick came in and said he was having a problem with an older couple and wanted Tony to "take care of it." Apparently, Dick had been a little pushy in trying to ram a new Impala down their throats. They wanted to talk to his manager.

I don't think Dick reached the outrageous level that car salesman Robert De Niro did in *Analyze That*. Facing a similar request, De Niro grabbed his crotch and shouted, "You want to see the manager? I'll show you the manager. Here's the manager!" Dick didn't grab anything but what he did do was equally offensive.

He directed the couple to the office of "Sales Manager" Tony, who of course, was no more the sales manager than I was the owner of the dealership; but he was a damn good actor. He listened intently to their complaints and then responded.

"First of all, I want to apologize on behalf of the entire dealership for my salesman's conduct. And I want to thank you for coming forward. I can't take back what happened. I can't undo what's been done. But I can tell you this. Today is Dick's last day. He's gone. I don't care how many kids he's got, how many personal problems. NOBODY — not at this dealership — gets away with treating customers like he treated you. NOBODY! And if you good folks never come back, never see fit to set foot in this dealership again, I'll understand. On the other hand, if you decide to ever give us one more chance, one more chance to make this right, you have my word, I will."

The elderly couple left. Dick came back into Tony's office. They both laughed hysterically and I learned about talking to managers.

Meanwhile, back at Crest Cadillac, the service manager wouldn't see me, neither would the general manager. I started walking through the dealership in search of ANYONE who would read my warranty. I might as well have been holding up *The Satanic Bible*. No one would even look at my booklet. I was asked to leave several times or to at least go to the customer lounge. I kept walking.

Eventually, I found a manager hiding in the parts department. He was aware of the whole incident. I showed him the warranty and asked him to read the page relating to tire coverage. He refused. Instead, he echoed that old refrain, "We don't cover tires. If you have a tire problem, go to Michelin."

I shouted back.

"I'm not going to Michelin. I bought a Cadillac. That Cadillac came with a 4 year/50,000 mile bumper-to-bumper warranty. That warranty covers tires. My tires are defective. Replace 'em."

Again, the familiar response. "Sir, go to Michelin."

I didn't go to Michelin, but I did leave the dealership, warning everyone within earshot, "I'll be back to take depositions." Two weeks later I returned with a court reporter to take those depositions for my lawsuit.

The human memory is amazingly short. The service writer who originally tried to sell me tires couldn't remember a thing — me, my car, the tires. Nothing. The parts manager who wouldn't read my warranty couldn't recall the incident. Now, the service manager told me that my tires were not defective. They were not cupping. There was no ply separation. In fact, he said, the reason my car pulled was not because of any factory defect at all. It pulled because I must have hit a curb. I must have done something to cause the pull. According to the dealer, IF I had a problem, I caused it.

Prior to this dealership runaround, I would have taken $40,000 to settle my case. But if this is how they were going to treat me, if this is what "Creating A Higher Standard" meant, somebody was going to pay. That somebody was General Motors. I held out for $62,500. Plus, GM paid $43,000 in attorney fees to my firm. All's well that ends well.

Afterthought

During the runaround, no one says anything about contacting your own representative, consulting an attorney to check out your legal rights. Nobody reminds consumers that they are dealing with the largest corporations on earth, corporations that will stop at nothing when it comes to money. They won't tell you, but I will.

The American Lemon

You look at a little car
and wonder how long it'll last.

The answers hidden deep inside.

— Ad for the Ford Pinto

From the minute it rolled into the showrooms of America, the Ford Pinto qualified as a lemon by ANY definition, ANY criteria, ANY standard. In truth and in fact, the Pinto was the MOTHER of all lemons. It was also an automotive atrocity that killed or horribly disfigured some of those who unknowingly made the mistake of buying the car.

Built under the direction of then Ford Vice President Lee Iacocca, the Pinto was introduced to the American car buying public in 1970. Iacocca has been credited with being the father of the Mustang, a truly original, all American car. His Pinto offspring would earn a different kind of fame.

The small, economic Pinto was Ford's entry into the new subcompact market and the competition from Volkswagen and the automotive manufacturers of Japan. The Pinto was sporty in design and in the bright colors of the '70s. Ads show the car in eye-popping orange, apple red and appropriately, lemon yellow. The price was just where Ford wanted it, under $2,000.

"Small bite," proclaimed the red-as-an-apple ad, "$1,919 (for so many miles of carefree driving)." The Madison Avenue boys were only half right. The driving would be anything but carefree.

In his autobiography, Iacocca, the man of many quotes, didn't show his usual zing when describing the Pinto. "Unhappily," he wrote in rare understatement, "the Pinto was involved in a number of accidents where the car burst into flames after a rear-end collision."

The question of how the Pinto got that way and stayed that way is still debated more than 30 years later. So are the ethics of the company responsible.

Death on Wheels

Unlike the ad claiming that the secret to the car's long life was hidden "deep inside," nobody had to look far to find the tragic flaw in the Pinto's design. It hung right out there for all to see.

"The next time you drive behind a Pinto... take a look at the rear end. That long silvery object hanging down under the bumper is the gas tank." Those words came from Mark Dowie in his article "Pinto Madness" in the September/October 1977 issue of *Mother Jones*. The article caused a national uproar and ultimately led to the Pinto recall in 1978 and the death of the "Pale Horse" in 1980. But, more importantly, for the first time all of America knew that the car had a problem — that gas tank.

With little between it and the chrome strip bumper, the tank would "buckle like an accordion, right up to the back seat," stated Dowie. All it took was a rear-end collision at 31 miles per hour and less. The tank could be punctured, the filler tube pulled out. Gas would spill. Sparks would ignite. The Pinto would explode and people would burn.

Dowie estimated that between 500 and 900 people died in such collisions. Ford had that figure much lower, perhaps as few as 25 fatalities between 1971–1976. The actual number will never be known, but somebody at Ford was counting during the Pinto years, counting costs and watching the clock.

They had rushed the Pinto through production. Dowie gave the average time to produce a new car as about 43 months. The Pinto was given 25 months. The race was on with the other subcompact contenders already out of the gate. During the production phase, crash tests took place. Fuel tanks ruptured and fuel spilled.

"If this 1969 crash test information is accurate," wrote Douglas Birsch, co-editor of *The Ford Pinto Case*, "Ford had adequate knowledge to make design changes in the Pinto fuel system prior to tooling."

One result of the testing, which continued after the Pinto was on the road, was the evidence that collision outcomes would change with minor modifications to the tank or fuel system. For instance, insert a rubber bladder in the gas tank for protection, move the tank over the axle, reinforce the bumper, and lives might be saved.

Once Ford knew it had a flaming coffin on its hands and a solution was available, why didn't it take immediate steps to correct the problem? It would only be moral and logical to do so. Could it have been the money?

Lee himself wrote, "… There's absolutely no truth to the charge that we tried to save a few bucks and knowingly made a dangerous car."

I'll take Lee at his word. Ford engineering did not DELIBERATELY set out to kill customers in firebombs. However, once it became apparent that "the carefree little American car" was a rolling inferno, Ford did nothing.

"For whatever reason," Birsch wrote, "Ford managers seem to have decided to allow people to die or to be injured who could have been saved from harm at a small cost…."

The cost to modify the Pinto would have been pitifully small on a car-by-car basis. Estimates have been given for possible modifications, repositioning the tank, rubber bladders, etc., from under $5 to $15.30. But there was that other cost to be considered by the bean counters, the value of a human life.

In 1972, the National Highway Traffic Safety Administration estimated human life to be worth $200,725. Where they got this number, God and Government only know. Ford rounded it out to $200,000.

Many believe that Ford did a "cost-benefit analysis" on the Pinto. This type of analysis balances the cost of a project against the financial benefit derived from the project. In the Pinto case, Ford would have balanced the cost of modifying the Pinto fuel system against the cost of lawsuits.

Using the available figures on the Pinto, we can do our own cost-benefit analysis. We'll go with the figure of 2,213,700 Pintos produced between 1971 and 1976 and the $11 modification cost often quoted. We too will put a $200,000 price tag on the value of a life in the 1970s.

By this analysis, if more than 121.75 people died in fiery Pinto crashes, Ford would derive a monetary benefit by making the $11 change. If less than 121 people burned to death in Pinto

Pinto Cost-Benefit Analysis

Cost

Pintos produced between 1971 and 1976	2,213,700
Modification cost per vehicle	x $11
Total cost of modification project	**$24,350,700**

Benefit

Cost of modification project	$24,350,700
Value of a human life	÷ $200,000
Deaths necessary to derive a financial benefit	**121.75**

explosions, Ford would derive no financial benefit from making the modifications.

It looks like "A BETTER IDEA" to fight death and injury lawsuits on a case-by-case basis, rather than modifying the fuel system. And remember, not everyone sues the Giant. And not everyone who sues the Giant wins.

You have to wonder how many Pinto drivers would have been willing to pay that extra $11 up front for the privilege of owning a 3-door lemon yellow Runabout that didn't explode when hit from behind. Unfortunately, they didn't get that option.

The Lawsuits

By 1978, about 50 lawsuits had been filed relative to the Pinto rear-end collisions. Some were settled out of court. Some were tried. One still makes news, the 1978 case of *Grimshaw v. Ford Motor Company.*

Richard Grimshaw was 13 years old when he was riding on a California freeway in a 1972 Ford Pinto driven by Lilly Gray. The car stalled and went up in flames when hit from behind by a 1962 Ford Galaxy at a reported speed of 28–37 miles per hour. Gray died from her burns. The boy Grimshaw lived with his, permanently disfigured. In its 2000 issue, *Trial*, the journal of the Association of Trial Lawyers of America, named the subsequent court case as one of the ten most important civil trials of the millennium.

Grimshaw and Gray's heirs sued Ford on the basis that Ford was aware of the fuel system design defect and willfully and deliberately failed to correct it. The jury agreed. Lilly Gray's heirs were awarded $659,680, but what caught the attention of the entire country was the verdict for the horribly burned Grimshaw. He was awarded $2.8 million in compensatory damages and an additional $125 million (reduced to $3.5 million by the trial court) in punitive damages.

Jeffrey Robert White, author of the *Trial* article wrote, "Juries do not design cars or issue safety standards. But they can draw a line against disregard for safety that companies ignore at their peril."

Ford appealed and lost.

The Fourth District Court of Appeals' comments were scathing:

> Through the results of the crash tests Ford knew that the Pinto's fuel tank and rear structure would expose consumers to serious injury or death in a 20 to 30 mile-per-hour collision. There was evidence that Ford could have corrected the hazardous design defects at minimal cost but decided to defer correction of the shortcomings by engaging in a cost-benefit analysis balancing human lives and limbs against corporate profit. Ford's institutional mentality was shown to be one of callous indifference to public safety. There was substantial evidence that Ford's conduct constituted "conscious disregard" of the probability of injury to members of the consuming public.

Long live Henry Ford and the Bottom Line!

A Dead Horse

The Ford Pinto was recalled in 1978 at a cost that may have run as high as $40 million. So much for saving money. In 1980, the Pinto was exterminated from the Ford line. The worst abomination in the history of American automotive engineering had finally come to an end.

Nothing before and nothing after has ever matched the Pinto. Yet, sadly, not one Pinto was ever bought back by Ford. Not one lawsuit was ever brought seeking a refund. Not one consumer had the option of returning the deathtrap. The Pinto WAS ahead of its time — 12 years to be exact. The first certifiable American Lemon had rolled off the assembly line 12 years BEFORE the first Lemon Law was enacted.

Afterthought

In 1996, a Ford E350 15-passenger van, with 13 people aboard, overturned on a Kentucky highway killing two passengers. In 1999, the wrongful death case of *Johnson v. Ford Motor Company* was filed in Federal District Court for the Northern District of Illinois. The plaintiffs alleged that the van was unsafe in handling and stability. They alleged that Ford knew it was unsafe because it had conducted computer generated mechanical system simulation rollover tests — also known as ADAMS modeling. Ford was accused of withholding evidence of such tests. Ford, of course, denied the accusations and claimed the van was safe.

On January 21, 2003 the Illinois District Court made the following Findings and Order:

> ... Defendant (Ford) has willfully concealed the existence of "ADAMS modeling" for the E350 15-passenger van, and has made numerous misrepresentations to this court and plaintiffs with respect to the existence of such modeling.
>
> Defendant is ordered to pay the reasonable attorneys' fees and costs incurred by plaintiffs in

connection with their various motions seeking the disclosure and production of ADAMS modeling.

Further, the judge stated that he would instruct the jury at trial that the computer-generated rollover tests demonstrated that the E350 van was unsafe in handling and stability. On February 22, 2003, 2 days before trial, Ford settled. As reported by the Associated Press, the judge stated that Ford's conduct "almost borders on criminal." Ford continues to face other lawsuits involving E350 van rollovers. **Some things never change**.

Lemon Law

*My car's a lemon. Those bastards
sold me a lemon. I painted it
yellow. Can I picket the dealer?
They're trying to arrest me.*

— Caller X

Last spring, I received a call from a frustrated woman in
Superior, Wisconsin, who wanted to know if I would be interested in taking her case. She had purchased a new Ford Mustang
in Minnesota. The car had paint problems — scratches, swirl
marks, discoloration. The dealer couldn't fix it. She skipped the
customer assistance runaround and went straight to the U.S.
Constitution. She picketed.

She covered herself with signs, handed out literature. She
pounded stakes into dealership property with slogans bad-
mouthing every descendant of Henry Ford. Things got so out of
control that a Minneapolis court issued a restraining order precluding her from going anywhere near the dealership for any
reason. If she handed out one more flyer, she'd go to jail.

I was intrigued by her story, but found her conduct
extreme and unnecessary. I dislike the Ford family as much as the
next guy, but no judge ever threatened me with prison over a
lemon. My caller was obviously a one-woman wrecking crew.

Lemons are problematic vehicles that haven't been
repaired. We don't have to paint them yellow. We don't have to

drive them through showroom windows or organize marches to Detroit in order to make a point. Outrageous conduct only diverts attention from the real issue. My caller had turned the focus on herself rather than the Mustang. That was a mistake.

I didn't take the case. I referred her to a good friend of mine, a Minnesota Lemon Law attorney. At one time, he had represented General Motors. I figured this case would be his penance for the sins he committed while defending Goliath.

State Lemon Laws

By the mid-1980s, every state had followed Connecticut's example by passing their own Lemon Law. This was good news for consumers, since Lemon Laws generally helped level the playing field between "David" and Detroit. The new laws were more effective and easier to understand than the Magnuson-Moss Act of 1975. They gave consumers explicit rights and ways to implement those rights. For the first time since the Model T rolled off the assembly line in 1908, David could stand toe-to-toe with the Giant. For the first time, consumers had laws with teeth. (For my rating of your state's Lemon Law, refer to the Appendix.)

Although specific provisions of each Lemon Law varied from state to state, the overall spirit was uniform. That spirit proclaimed, "If Detroit sells me a lemon, I can give it back. I'm not stuck with it like in the old days. I don't have to trade it in or sell it to some unsuspecting chump. If it's a lemon, Detroit owes me a refund, or a new car."

Basic Coverage

Every state Lemon Law applies to new vehicles used primarily for personal, family, or household purposes. Your Toyota

Camry and Honda Civic are covered, no doubt about it. Some states go further. They include motorcycles, motor homes, semi-trucks, even motorized wheelchairs, in their Lemon Laws. Some states cover business vehicles and some don't. Demonstrators, executive driven and leased vehicles typically have protection. Used cars typically don't. Only a handful of states have adopted used car Lemon Laws. Hopefully, this will change.

Write to your state representative. We desperately need help with the "Have I got a deal for you" mentality of the used car lot.

Now, what makes that car a Lemon?

The Nonconformity

Nonconformity is a ten-dollar law school word for problem. It appears in every state Lemon Law. State legislators drafted every state Lemon Law. Many legislators are lawyers and lawyers don't like calling a problem a problem. Problem is too simple a word. Far too many people understand its meaning. Lawyers like to use words that only other lawyers understand. They spent too much time and money in law school to use simple words. Lawyers don't say, "I'm having a problem with my car," or "My car has a problem." Lawyers say:

> Please be advised, that subsequent to taking delivery as a lessor, under the terms of a closed end consumer lease obligation, the said vehicle being the subject of said obligation, gradually manifested a nonconformity, that hereby continues to date.

There you have it. We are all stuck with the term "nonconformity" because it takes seven years to get a law degree.

Most state Lemon Laws define nonconformity as a condition or defect that substantially impairs the use, value OR safety of a motor vehicle and is covered by an express warranty, but does not include a condition or defect caused by abuse, neglect, or unauthorized modification. Simply put, if your vehicle has a substantial problem that's covered by warranty, and you didn't cause the problem, you have a nonconformity.

Some states require the nonconformity to cause substantial impairment of use AND value. Others require only the value of the vehicle to be substantially impaired. No matter what state you're in, a substantial impairment of SOMETHING is necessary. Substantial is a subjective term. The auto industry and I differ on its definition.

For Detroit, everything's minor. Nothing is substantial except corporate executive pension plans. Trunk leaks, door rattles, vibrations, exploding gas tanks, nothing rises to the level of nonconformity. However, I don't want my trunk to leak. I don't want my doors to rattle. I don't want my transmission to slip — even a little. And, if it does, that's substantial to me. By my definition and good sense, that car has a nonconformity.

Reasonable Number of Repair Attempts

Just having a nonconformity isn't enough to force a buy-back under state Lemon Laws. If my Corvette stalls in traffic, I can't take a cab to the nearest Chevy dealer and pick out a new Z06. GM gave me a WARRANTY, not a GUARANTEE. They promised to fix my car if I had problems. They didn't promise that I wouldn't have problems. If my car stalls in traffic, they get a chance to fix it. If it stalls again, they get another chance. However, this can't go on forever.

Lemon Laws limit the number of chances the manufacturer gets to correct a problem. If my nonconformity isn't repaired within a reasonable number of attempts, I get the new Corvette. How many tries does Detroit get? What is reasonable? Unfortunately, 50 states have come up with some 40 different definitions of what constitutes a reasonable number of repair attempts. Nobody wants to make this too easy.

Most Lemon Laws give the manufacturer three or four chances within a specified time period to repair a single non-conformity — 12 months/12,000 miles, 18 months/18,000 miles, 24 months/24,000 miles or some other combination of time and mileage. If the problem deemed a nonconformity isn't repaired within the prescribed time limit, the vehicle is a lemon. In a few states, one or two repair attempts are enough if the nonconformity "results in a complete failure of the braking or steering system and is likely to cause death or serious bodily injury."

The second way of calculating reasonable number of repair attempts deals with "days out of service." This refers to the total number of days, not consecutive, a vehicle sits in the shop for ANY warranty nonconformity repairs. Most Lemon Laws have determined that 30 days in the shop — some say calendar, others business — within a defined time period, is unreasonable. Meaning, if my Corvette is out of service for a total of 30 or more days within the first year of delivery, regardless of the problems, I'm going to get that new yellow C6 convertible.

It doesn't matter if they finally fix the problem on the fifth, sixth or seventh repair shop visit. The car is a lemon. Why should your car sit in the shop for 30 days? Why should you spend months, if not years, taking your car in for repairs? They had their chance. They should have fixed it the first time, maybe the second, but not the seventh. You don't have to put up with their inefficiency or indifference.

Lemon-aid

Once we've established a nonconformity and failure to repair within a reasonable number of attempts, the rest is easy, a cakewalk. Just write a letter to Detroit. Tell them you have a lemon. Request a refund or replacement. Send it certified. Wait four weeks. Walk to the mailbox. Pick up your refund check. Deposit it in the bank. Go shopping for a new car. If you requested a replacement vehicle, drive to your dealer. Drop off your lemon. Inspect your new car. Drive it home.

Now, if by some strange quirk, you don't get what you ask for, you can either give up or sue. I prefer the latter.

Attorney Fees

It's been my experience that most Lemon Law lawyers don't charge their clients if they lose the case. They go into a lawsuit believing they will win and their fees will be covered by the losing side, the automotive manufacturer.

I don't work for General Motors. I'm not employed by Nissan and I've never interviewed with DaimlerChrysler. I hate Ford. I don't like KIA and I'm not fond of Honda. Yet, because of the Lemon Law, these companies pay me, Vince Megna of Waukesha, Wisconsin, $225 an hour to sue them, to take them to court. In fact, they pay me more money than they pay their own attorneys. It's almost sadistic. It's almost better than a government job. AND I CAN'T BE FIRED! As I gloat, remember this: the attorney fee provision of Lemon Law is an absolute necessity for the consumer.

Most, but not all state Lemon Laws require Detroit to pay the consumer's attorney fees, if the consumer wins. As was true in Magnuson-Moss, without the attorney fee provision Lemon Laws are worthless. The cost of litigation is too high for both the consumer and the attorney.

Legal fees can run $25,000, $50,000 even $100,000 in contested Lemon Law cases. If the manufacturer didn't have to pay those fees, no one would ever sue. Who in their right mind would pay some lawyer $25,000 or more to have a $20,000 Jeep Liberty bought back? NOBODY. If the manufacturer didn't have to pay those fees, we'd just keep our lemons, or trade them in.

That would make Detroit happy. And, in some states, that is exactly what happens.

The Nine

Eight states — Alaska, Illinois, Kansas, Montana, Nevada, North Dakota, Oklahoma, Texas — and Washington D.C. make no provision for attorney fees. I'm disappointed with these states. No, **appalled** would be a better word. At least Nevada is not hypocritical. With legalized prostitution, everybody gets screwed in Nevada. In the other states just the car buyers get screwed.

Citizens of The Nine either forget about their car trouble or file claims under Magnuson-Moss. Yes, the same piece of legislation that proved ineffective in the 70s, the one that made a new generation of Lemon Laws necessary, has returned. In eight states and D.C., millions of Americans have to rely on something that barely worked in 1975 to fight the auto industry of the 21st century.

Detroit loves The Nine.

Three More

Three more states — Missouri, Hawaii and Colorado — seem to have written their Lemon Laws with a little help from their friends in Detroit.

In Missouri, the "Show Me State," if Detroit makes me a settlement offer prior to commencing a lawsuit and I don't take it and I sue, I must recover at least 10 percent more than that offer. If not, I "shall be liable for all costs and reasonable attorney's fees incurred by the manufacturer."

Meaning, if the total damages related to my lemon are $20,000 and Detroit offers me $18,200, I have no choice. I have to take it. If I sue and get the full $20,000, the amount I am entitled to UNDER THE LAW, I will have to pay Detroit's costs and attorney fees because my recovery falls under a 10 percent improvement of Detroit's original offer. I might not be the smartest guy in the world, but paying $80,000 in fees to get $1,800 doesn't make sense. I'll eat the loss. Missouri has shown me.

Hawaii is a beautiful place. The mountains. The ocean. Don Ho's Island Grill. I just don't want to buy a car there. I'll rent. If I have a lemon in Hawaii, I must submit my dispute to either a binding or non-binding state run arbitration program.

If I choose binding, I'm stuck with the decision. If I lose, I may have to pay the manufacturer's attorney fees. If I choose non-binding and don't like the decision, I can go to court. BEWARE of the Hawaiian courtroom.

If I don't improve my position in court "by at least 25 PERCENT," I have to pay the manufacturer's costs and attorney fees. I'd do better at the beach or back in Missouri.

And finally, Colorado. The worst of the worst. The baddest of the bad. Detroit is immune from Lemon Law prosecution in the Rocky Mountains. If you sue Ford under the Colorado Lemon Law and lose, you pay Ford's attorney fees, no ifs, ands or buts about it. In Colorado, "The court SHALL award reasonable attorney fees to THE PREVAILING SIDE in any action brought to enforce the provisions of this article (Lemon Law)." Consumers don't sue in Colorado because they can't take the chance of losing.

One of my favorite books is *Letters from a Nut* by Ted L. Nancy. The book contains 82 insanely bizarre and preposterous letters from Nancy, the nut, to corporations, hotels, politicians, and the like. In these letters, Nancy creates unbelievable scenarios that could not possibly be taken seriously by anyone "in their right mind."

He becomes a hotel guest who travels with an 8' by 3' breakable mirror, a double for Abraham Lincoln requesting a presidential suite, the 2-foot 3-inch PIP THE MIGHTY SQUEAK seeking employment with Ringling Brothers. The responses Ted receives — included in the book — show just how many people are NOT in their right mind.

In a strange Nancyesque twist, I have recently discovered a letter written by anti-consumer advocate H.P. Larredan to the Governor of Colorado. The difference between Mr. Nancy and Mr. Larredan is that the spirit of Mr. Larredan's letter speaks the truth:

H. P. Larredan
Anti-consumer Advocate
700-Q University Blvd. S
P. M. Box 104
Mobile, Alabama 36609

September 1, 2003

The Honorable Bill Owens
Governor of the State of Colorado
136 State Capitol
Denver, Colorado 80203-1792

Dear Governor Owens:

I am the founding member of KCD (Keep the Consumer Down), a private organization that supports gorged corporate profits at any cost. KCD also supports all efforts to keep the "little guy" in his place.

Each year we recognize the American corporation or governmental body whose action or leadership exemplifies the *Stick It to You* principles on which KCD is founded. We are extremely proud of past recipients including Arthur Anderson, WorldCom, ImClone, Tyco, and of course, Enron. Unfortunately, many of these great companies are no longer in business. But at least they stood up to the consumer.

This year you have been chosen to receive the KCD award in recognition of Colorado's useless and ineffective Lemon Law. Proudly, Colorado can boast of having the worst Lemon Law in the country. Your state is the only state in the Union to make the consumer pay the auto manufacturer's attorney fees if the consumer sues and loses. This is truly a tribute to your leadership and the legislators of Colorado. In this day of "whiney consumerism," it is hard enough to shut the "little guy" up, let alone keep him down. Colorado has done an exemplary job in burying the "little guy" and keeping corporate profits high.

As a result, the Colorado Lemon Law gives the overwhelming advantage to the already almighty industry. Citizens of Colorado with car trouble are basically screwed. They are scared shitless of suing the auto industry and remain at the merciless mercy of Detroit. This is good!

In recognition and appreciation of Colorado's unending anti-consumerism mentality, KCD takes great pride in presenting you with this year's award — A 14-CARAT-GOLD-PLATED 24:1 SCALE REPLICA OF THE 1973 FORD PINTO THREE DOOR HATCHBACK.

Sincerely,

H. P. Larredan
Anti-consumer Advocate

My Lemons

*I have good news and I have
bad news: Your car is a lemon.*

— **Vince Megna**

Between 1997 and 2001, I bought five new cars. All five were lemons. All five were bought back by Detroit. The odds of having five lemons in a row are 48,000,000 to 1. I should either put my money into lottery tickets or never leave the house. Depending on how you look at it.

The Cadillac

In the old days, if you drove a Cadillac, it meant something. You were Italian, a drug dealer or pimp, or some combination thereof. Today, Cadillac is just another car. It has no identity. However, I have a soft spot in my heart for Detroit's first luxury automobile. My first lemon was a Cadillac.

The 1997 Cadillac Sedan DeVille didn't meet the "Higher Standard" General Motors advertised. No "BREAKTHROUGH" here. It pulled and vibrated. The brakes were bad. The door locks jammed, locking me outside on a freezing January night with the engine running. I took it to dealers in Jacksonville, Florida, Nashville, Tennessee, and Fayetteville, Arkansas, but nobody could fix it. I sued GM and settled for $62,500 plus $47,000 in attorney fees.

The Concorde

When my wife and I stopped at the Chrysler dealership we weren't planning to buy a car. We were just looking. I like to visit the showroom from time to time to keep up on the current bullshit. Connie likes to visit the showroom because they sell cars. How odd.

Joe T., our friendly salesman, greeted us. It was June 27, 1998. You know what That means. The month is almost over. If I don't buy today and take delivery by the thirtieth, I'll never get this deal again. All the incentives run out at the end of the month. What Mr. T didn't say was that they all start up again on the first of next month. Still, I went along. Who am I to question?

Joe showed us around. He explained the benefits of new car "investment" and how leasing gives the option of returning a vehicle after 36 months without further obligation. I didn't challenge Joe's wisdom. After all, he's been on the sales floor for almost a year. Then he showed us a 1998 burgundy Concorde. It looked good. Connie liked it. We agreed to a test drive.

And I thought my lemon Cadillac had pulled badly. It was nothing compared to this car. Anything on the right was a target — curb, ditch, mailbox — you name it. Chrysler wouldn't be able to fix this. Not in a couple of tries, anyway. It was perfect for me. I like a good lemon. I get to drive it for free until I get a replacement or refund.

We returned to the dealership and we did talk about the pulling. Joe assured me that it was nothing. "All cars pull until they get broken in," he explained. "Besides, Chrysler has one of the best warranties in the business." I could bring the car back anytime for a warranty alignment.

Well, that works for me. If they all pull, why look elsewhere? I'd have the same trouble with Lexus, Mercedes, or KIA. We signed the contract. Connie was the proud owner of a new Chrysler Concorde. One year later, we returned it for a full refund.

The Corvette

If I could own any car in the world, it would be an Enzo Ferrari. My next choice would be a Chevy Corvette.

When I went to pick up my 2000 Corvette, it wouldn't start. The dealer had to jump it. Dale, my salesman, looked embarrassed, but explained that it was quite common for new cars not to start. This sounded a lot like our old friend Joe T. According to Dale, the problem had something to do with electronics. I guess for 56,000 bucks you can't expect perfection. Anyway, I wasn't worried. I had 24-hour roadside assistance and the Lemon Law.

As I was leaving, the general manager came over and handed me his home phone number in case of trouble over the weekend. I thought that was very considerate. His last words were, "Vince, don't lemon this on me. We'll take care of you." Wow, I hadn't owned this car an hour and the "L" word had already come up.

I never did have any more trouble starting the 'vette. Maybe Dale was right. Maybe brand new cars just don't start. However, I had other issues — brakes, grinding noises, water leaks, false readings on the Driver Information Center and a bad rear differential. The car was in the shop over 30 days during the first year. I filed a Lemon Law claim. GM accepted my offer. A couple of months later, the same general manager who told me not to lemon it was handing me the keys to a new 2002 Millennium Yellow Corvette.

The new 'vette has proven to be problem-free — except for an engine knock. That's quite a tribute. I don't know to what exactly, but it's quite a tribute.

The Mustangs

According to a 1976 Federal Trade Commission sponsored survey, 30 percent of new automobiles were sold with defects.

Twenty-three years later, I was ahead of the survey. Sixty-six percent of my new cars had defects. And that percentage was about to increase.

It was time for my son's first new car. He was seventeen and his grandpa wanted to give him a birthday present. We ordered the car of his choice, a 1999 yellow Mustang. I was impressed with his color selection. Yellow is such an important part of my life. I was proud to see that the seed does not fall far from the tree. A couple of weeks later, we went to the dealership to take delivery and found a problem waiting for us. The Mustang had frame damage.

The service manager put the car on a rack and pointed out a big dent in the frame under the front passenger area. It looked like it had been sledge-hammered. He told us the problem could be repaired by drilling a hole through the front floorboard and attaching a metal type brace to reinforce the frame. I was thinking, you gotta be kidding. This is insane. You guys are all crazy. This car is dangerous. It's structurally unsound. I'm not going to let my son drive this.

I told the manager, "We can't accept it. Why would Ford even let me take a car with frame damage?" The dealer didn't push it. They would try to locate another yellow Mustang.

The second Mustang arrived about ten days later. This time the frame was okay, but the transmission leaked and clunked. It took seven visits to the repair shop within the first year to fix it. Under the Wisconsin Lemon Law, if the problem is not repaired by the fourth attempt, you have a claim. At one repair visit, we were handed two quarts of Motorcraft MERCON V Automatic Transmission Fluid and told to check the level every fifty miles, adding when necessary. This just wasn't acceptable. We filed.

About two and a half years after the first Mustang was turned down because of frame damage, Ford bought back the second one for $25,000, plus attorney fees. So far I'm four for four.

The 300M

As a replacement for the Lemon Concorde, Connie bought the 1999 Motor Trend car of the year — the Chrysler 300M. Of all my Lemons, this was the weakest. There was a "nibble" in the steering wheel. The car had a slight vibration. I sent a demand to DaimlerChrysler just to see their response. How wimpy is this company? It should have been rejected. I wouldn't have sued.

There was no resistance. They gave me the royal treatment. To paraphrase Chrysler's response:

> Thank you for your demand, Mr. Megna. Daimler-Chrysler is always pleased to buy back your defective vehicles. Would you like a refund, or replacement? And again, thank you for not suing us. We'll reserve our screwing for the people without lawyers.

We picked out a new 2002 300M which, surprisingly, runs reasonably well. I think it has a slight drift to the left, but Connie won't take it in.

My cases weren't settled so easily because of Detroit's fondness for me. In fact, I don't have many friends in Detroit — maybe none. No one at General Motors ever said, "Let's give Vince Megna a new Corvette. He deserves it." Nobody has ever suggested, "Why don't we buy back Megna's $38,000 DeVille for $107,000? It's the least we can do."

No, Chrysler has never sent me an invitation saying, "Lease our cars free. No money down. No interest. No payments — *ever!* Consider this a token of Dieter Zetsche's appreciation." My cases settled because I'm a lawyer, and Detroit has a double standard where members of the bar are concerned.

The Double Standard

> **Double Standard:** ... a set of
> principles that applies differently
> and more rigorously to one group
> of people or circumstances than
> to another....
>
> **— Merriam-Webster Dictionary**

Forget the dictionary. In Detroit, Michigan, the double standard means: if you don't have a lawyer, you're screwed.

Most people I've met are scared to death of Small Claims Court. They couldn't collect the 300 bucks they lent their brother-in-law at last year's Christmas party. Yet, somehow they are led to believe that they can negotiate with Ford Motor Company or talk DaimlerChrysler into a settlement. Think again. Some old man from North Dakota isn't going to intimidate General Motors. Neither is some young man. When the average Joe tells Detroit, "I've got a lemon but no lawyer," Detroit tells Joe, "THANK YOU."

Rejection

Detroit's second response to "I'm going it alone" is to DENY:

> We have reviewed the repair history of your vehicle
> and based on the available information we are unable

to comply with your request for repurchase. At Ford Motor Company, we commit substantial resources to satisfying our customers.... However, limits must be placed on those efforts.

At this time, Volkswagen is not in a position to make a settlement offer.

While we regret any inconvenience you may have experienced, the circumstances do not justify the repurchase of your vehicle under the Lemon Law... please be assured that we will continue to honor our commitment under the terms of the Mercedes-Benz New Vehicle Limited Warranty.

Putting it another way:

Pound sand. Take a hike. Get screwed!

If you won't do any of the above, Detroit then tries to give you next to nothing.

Goodwill

In Sicily, it's called Ice. In Detroit, it's called Goodwill. Either way, it's almost nothing and the story is always the same:

Your car doesn't qualify. It's not a lemon. It doesn't meet the standard but we want to give you something anyway. We want to give you an extended warranty so you can bring your car in for another 25,000 miles. We want to give you an Owner Appreciation Certificate worth $1,500 towards the purchase of your next car. We want to give you $2,000 in cash for your inconvenience. All you have to do to get any one of these generous offers — remember you're entitled to nothing — is sign a simple release giving up all your rights.

Think about this. If you were really entitled to nothing, why would Detroit give you ANYTHING? It's hard enough getting a free car wash today. But don't take my word for it. Call General Motors at 1-800-222-1020. Tell them you've been a loyal customer for 25 years. Request an extended warranty on your Monte Carlo in the name of customer relations.

Call Chrysler. Explain how you got laid off and money is tight. This is the same company that was bailed out by the United States Government in 1979. They should understand. See if they will make next month's Neon payment for you.

Drive up to a Ford dealership. Tell them you're due for an oil change but short on cash. Ask if, just this once, you could get a "goodwill" oil change. My guess is that any gesture you receive will not be in the nature of goodwill.

The Buyback

Even the blind squirrel gets a nut now and then. Sometimes the vehicle is so bad, so clearly a lemon, that Detroit has no choice. They have to buy it back. But Detroit is still a thief, worse than any mugger on the street.

On the street, you know when you're being robbed. The mugger comes up, pulls a gun, pulls a knife, and takes your money. You've been robbed. Detroit doesn't pull a gun. Detroit doesn't say, "Hand over your money, bitch," but Detroit does start talking and thieving the minute a buyback looks inevitable.

Detroit tells you that you have to pay the Manufacturer's Suggested Retail Price difference between your lemon and the current model. **You don't**. There will be an upgrade fee.

There isn't. The reasonable use charge is $2,400. **It's $350**. Detroit says, "We can't reimburse you for finance charges, lease payments, or rentals." **They can**.

Detroit is a street thug in corporate clothing. I have more respect for the street thug. At least, he's honest.

The Sara Johnson Story

Sara Johnson got screwed so bad they put her picture in a magazine. Her story was told in the September 2001 issue of *Kiplinger's Personal Finance*.

Sara paid sticker price for a 1998 KIA Sephia. That was her first mistake. At least she bought in 1998. *Consumer Reports'* April 1999 review warned, "You'd have to search far and wide to find a car that's worse than this small Korean model."

For Sara, the search was over. Her Sephia had major engine problems — fault codes, defective wiring, fuel pump recalls, an improperly machined flywheel. The car wouldn't start. When it did start, it stalled. This Sephia was a single mom's nightmare.

KIA dealers worked on the engine 11 times and still couldn't fix it. In frustration, Sara contacted KIA Motor America WITHOUT an attorney. That was her second mistake.

A KIA representative told Sara that, according to company analysis, her Sephia didn't meet the Lemon Law standard. It didn't qualify for a buyback. They were wrong, of course. The Wisconsin Lemon Law doesn't say four repair attempts for GM, twelve for KIA, but I understand KIA's position. If that company had to take back every Sephia that was in the shop 11 times, they'd go bankrupt, just like Daewoo. And that wouldn't be right, would it?

The rep did have one piece of good news for the lawyerless Sara. Because of KIA's undying commitment to customer satisfaction, they would reimburse Sara for four car payments —

KIA and *Consumer Reports*

Consumer Reports is a non-profit publication that accepts no advertising and renders unbiased opinions on consumer products. This is what *Consumer Reports* has to say about KIA:

May 1999 — Sephia. The Sephia has little to recommend it. It rides harshly even on smooth roads. Pavement flaws elicit sharp jerks, and bumpy corners knock the car off course. The engine booms coarsely, especially during acceleration, and the cabin is never quiet.

September 1999 — Sportage. The Sportage delivers just about the nastiest ride of any passenger vehicle made today. Road bumps transmit hard shocks, making the body bound like a pogo stick. You're also treated to grating road, wind, and engine noise.

April 2000 — Sephia. You'd have to search far and wide to find a car that's worse than this small Korean Model. The ride is awful. The cabin is noisy, the powertrain is crude and unrefined, and handling is clumsy.

April 2001 — Sportage. This small, unrefined SUV trails just about any car in its class. The Sportage's trucklike body-on-frame construction contributes to its rough ride. Handling is clumsy, with lots of body lean, and the powertrain is crude, slow, and noisy.

April 2002 — Spectra. You'd have to search far and wide to find a worse new car than the Spectra.... Engineering miscues abound, from a pernicious, scalp-gashing trunklid latch to doors that are prone to swinging shut when the car is parked on an incline. The Spectra sedan also received poor offset-crash-test scores from the IIHS.

April 2002 — Sportage. When it comes to small, truck-based SUV's, this primitive model is among the worst of an unimpressive lot. The ride is stiff and jittery, and handling is clumsy, with slow steering and lots of body lean.... Depreciation is high.

April 2003 — Rio. The Rio is one of the lowest-priced cars sold in the U.S. Expect to get what you pay for. It is based on the dreadful Ford Aspire, which was made for Ford by Kia in the mid-1990s.

$1,131.72 — as a one-time goodwill gesture for her inconvenience. All she had to do was sign a release giving up her rights to ever make a claim against KIA or any of its subsidiaries. It was so easy. Sara accepted the payments and signed the release. That was her third mistake.

Generally, when you sign a release, the case is over. Still, when Sara called and explained what happened, I felt KIA's conduct was so unconscionable that it couldn't go unchecked. KIA took unfair advantage of a consumer, forced her to keep an inherently defective car that THEY BUILT and gave her next to nothing in exchange for the release. We took the case and filed suit.

The Court threw out the release. It was "void as a waiver of plaintiff's rights under the Wisconsin lemon law." Most states have similar provisions precluding waiver of Lemon Law rights. Sara Johnson was entitled to her day in court, but a trial wasn't necessary. KIA decided to cut its losses.

On May 23, 2001, the case settled. KIA paid Sara $27,288 for her $14,000 Sephia, plus $24,000 in attorney fees. In addition, she kept the $1,131.72 one-time "goodwill gesture."

Ken Peterson

Ken Peterson's story is another example of the unscrupulous double standard that lives in the industry. It was one of the strongest cases I've ever handled.

Ken kept the greens at the University of Wisconsin — Green Bay golf course. His 2000 Ford Mustang was a summertime dream, but Packerland winters are brutal on rear wheel drives. Dodge looked like the answer. On a blizzardy January 17, 2001, Ken traded his favorite car for a Ram 1500 pickup. At last, snow would no longer be a problem. Regrettably, a Dodge engine would take its place.

Twenty days after delivery, at 650 miles, Ken checked the oil. It was black and a half-quart low. He immediately drove to the dealership. The service manager didn't have an answer. He shook his head and suggested that an oil change would take care of the problem.

Five days later, an odd squeaking sound started coming from the dash. The windshield was separating from the body. Can you believe this? It took eight days to get it resealed.

For the next two months, the Ram seemed fine. At 2,900 miles, however, the oil looked awfully dirty again. Why was this oil so filthy in so few miles? Seven hundred miles later, the windshield didn't fit and the engine had a rough idle. Back to the shop for the third time.

The dealer wrote on the repair order, "Monitored misfires and noticed a few on every cylinder.... Looked at new truck with the same motor and it idles the same as this one."

Obviously, Ken Peterson didn't know what he was talking about. If two Dodge trucks misfire on every cylinder, then all Dodge trucks misfire on every cylinder — Philosophy of Automotive Logic 101.

Oddly enough, I can't recall even one DaimlerChrysler commercial mentioning that all Dodge Rams misfire on every cylinder. I'll be sure to keep a closer watch during next year's Super Bowl.

Ken's truck was in the shop for seven more days. He took it home. The next day he was back at the shop. Now the Ram had a loud ratcheting lifter noise. The engine still ran rough and the oil had been overfilled and was overflowing.

The dealer acknowledged, "Anybody can make a mistake of adding too much oil." I'm sure that's why the oil pan comes equipped with a drain plug. As far as the noise and rough idle, the technician did not hear any ticking and the "engine ran fine." I wonder if this was the same tech who couldn't see the full line on the dipstick.

About four weeks later, at 4,339 miles, "the whiner" was back again, this time complaining of a rough idle and lifter noise. How many times does this guy have to be told that these are "characteristics" of Dodge trucks? Greens keeper Ken had apparently stopped a few too many golf balls with his head. Knowing nothing was wrong, the dealer performed the "Customer is Always Right," inspection.

A *slight* problem was verified, "mechanical failure within the lifters." Valve tappets were replaced resulting in a "quieter, smoother operation." Maybe this guy would finally be satisfied.

One month later, "HE'S BACK."

This time the technician was able to find a clearance problem with the number four cylinder and confirmed a ticking noise. The engine was removed — actually taken out of the truck — and a new short block was ordered. Twenty-four days later, Ken picked up his Ram with the new block. He should have been overjoyed. Not just anyone can get Chrysler to drop in a new engine after only 5,477 miles. (I wonder if all Dodge Rams will now be getting new engines to correct the misfire characteristic?)

The vehicle ran reasonably well for a whopping six weeks. That would normally make any consumer happy, and Ken proved to be no exception. Then, the tick came back. It took our geniuses at the repair facility an additional seven days to figure out that the timing chain tensioner was bent and hitting the cover. This crew might do very well on a "Where's Waldo" quiz. At that point, the Ram had been in the shop for 54 days between January 17 and October 15, 2001.

In Wisconsin, if a vehicle has nonconformities that cause it to be out of service for 30 or more days, you've got yourself a lemon. How could a bad engine not be substantial? Have you ever had a windshield fly off at 80 miles per hour? It's not a pretty sight. Fifty-four is more than 30. The Dodge Ram met the criteria.

Ken didn't think he needed a lawyer. He contacted the state for information on how to proceed. The Department of

Transportation sent him a Lemon Law brochure along with a "Lemon Law Notice" form. Ken filled out the form and mailed two copies by certified mail. One copy went to DaimlerChrysler Motors Corporation, the other to the National Center for Dispute Settlement (NCDS), the arbitration program used by Chrysler. In addition, making sure to cover all bases, the greens keeper called DaimlerChrysler and verbally requested a refund.

To Ken's surprise, Chrysler did not respond to either his letter or his phone call. The only response came from the NCDS. They mailed Ken's Lemon Law Notice back to him, stating, "we are not the proper forum to hear and decide a 'Lemon Law' dispute." Put less diplomatically, they told Ken, "Go fish in the Fox River."

Chrysler's conduct was the double standard in its purest form. Because Ken didn't have a lawyer, he was treated as if he didn't exist. Had my office sent out the original notice, Ken's lemon would have been bought back within 30 days. ABSOLUTELY NO DOUBT ABOUT IT! The same industry that gave me five buybacks in a row, gave Ken that Italian salute. Well, now he did have a lawyer and this lawyer filed a lawsuit on December 15, 2001.

Six months later, DaimlerChrysler came crawling on its corporate knees begging to settle. I like to see the Giant beg. They offered a refund. You scum, I thought, this guy has been in this mess for a year, had his truck sitting in the shop 54 days, writes two letters, calls Chrysler, gets a next-to-nothing response and the best you can do is offer him a refund? I was furious. I can still hear the rage in my voice when I made the call.

"We will not accept one penny less than 1.75 times single damages ($35,000), plus attorney fees. That is the bottom line. TAKE IT OR LEAVE IT. We will not negotiate. If that's not acceptable, you don't have to call back. We'll see you in court!"

We didn't see Chrysler in court. They paid. They had no choice.

Fresno, California — 2001

In 2001, a Fresno, California jury, punished, really punished, Ford Motor Company.

The original owner of a 1997 Ford Taurus had transmission trouble. He went to Ford on his own seeking a buyback under California's Lemon Law. He didn't get it. Instead, Ford gave him a $1,500 "Owner Appreciation Certificate" and told him to trade in the Taurus at a local dealer. He did. The dealer turned around and sold the Taurus to Jo Ann and Greg Johnson.

Within a few months, the Johnsons had transmission problems. Within 15 months, the transmission had been replaced twice. Originally, when the Johnsons looked at the Taurus, they asked to see its repair history. The dealer said there was none. Now, they went back to the dealer and demanded the repair history. This time they got it. Greg and Jo Ann were outraged. Ford knew about the transmission trouble all along, but kept it quiet. The Johnsons called Ford.

As usual, Ford was Ford. They wouldn't buy the car back. Nothing could be done. Still, in the spirit of goodwill, in the spirit of customer relations, Ford was willing to offer the Johnsons an extended warranty. This would cover the Taurus in case the transmission problem continued. The Johnsons would only have to pay a small deductible at each future repair visit. Such a deal. Fortunately, Jo Ann and Greg didn't think so. They hired an attorney in California.

A lawsuit was filed alleging the Taurus was a de facto lemon and that Ford should have disclosed the transmission problem. Ford said there was nothing to disclose. The car was never a lemon. It was never a buyback. The Owner Appreciation Certificate given to the previous owner was simply a goodwill gesture.

Evidence at trial showed that Ford gave out an average of 1,300 of these goodwill certificates a year to people who claimed "lemon." And that was just in California. According to the Johnson's attorney, William Krieg, every time Ford gave out a certificate instead of buying the lemon back, they saved between $6,000 and $10,000. Explained Krieg, "The cost-benefit analysis for Ford showed that the practice was too compelling to stop."

The jury didn't appreciate Ford's conduct. The Taurus WAS a lemon. The car should have been bought back from the original owner, whether he had a lawyer or not. The Owner Appreciation Certificate was a slap in the face. Unfortunately, nothing could be done for the first owner. He had accepted the "goodwill gesture" and was out of the picture. However, something could be done for the Johnsons. Ford could be FORCED to buy back the Taurus, but would that be enough? Would a simple buyback send a clear message to the auto industry? No. At least, the jury didn't think so.

In addition to ordering a buyback in the sum of $17,812, the jury awarded **$10,000,000** in punitive damages to Jo Ann and Greg. At the time of publication, the case was on appeal, but I still like California.

The Test

Over the past several years, I have enjoyed testing manufacturers on their commitment to the double standard. In conducting The Test, I help a client fill out a Lemon Law Demand Notice. The client then signs the notice and sends it to Detroit. My name does not appear. Detroit thinks the consumer is lawyer-free, acting on his or her own.

We monitor each test case closely to see if the "non-represented client" continues to be treated differently than a "represented client." Detroit always fails the test with flying colors. Time and time again, the consumer going it alone is turned down, offered next to nothing or not even acknowledged. The Double Standard lives.

Double Standard Test Form (Page 1 of 2)

Motor Vehicle Lemon Law Notice
Demand for relief under s. 218.0171, Wisconsin Statutes
Print & complete, or click on first line. Tab to next field. Enter only as much text as will fit on a line.

Pursuant to the Wisconsin Lemon Law, I am notifying __FORD MOTOR COMPANY__ of the following:
(check one)   *manufacturer*

☑ My vehicle has been made available for repair at least 4 times for the same defect during its first year of warranty.

☑ My vehicle has been out of service at least 30 days because of one or more defects during its first year of warranty.

Vehicle make __FORD__ Model __FOCUS SE__ Year __2001__ VIN (17 digits) ▓▓▓▓▓▓▓▓

Name and city/state of selling or leasing dealer or leasing company __HEISER FORD, MILWAUKEE, WISCONSIN__

Date of vehicle delivery __AUGUST 7, 2001__ Today's date __AUGUST 23, 2002__

Name of financial institution that financed/leased vehicle __FORD MOTOR CREDIT COMPANY__ Loan account # ▓▓▓▓▓▓
By providing this information, I authorize the manufacturer to contact this financial institution for financing information needed to calculate a refund. Authorization expires 35 days after the date of this form.

→ See back for vehicle defect and repair information ←

My vehicle has a defect(s) that substantially impairs its use, value or safety. I demand that the manufacturer give me *one* of the following within 30 days:
(check one)
☑ A comparable new vehicle in accordance with the Lemon Law, plus collateral costs
☐ A refund calculated in accordance with the Lemon Law, plus collateral costs

Description of collateral costs I have incurred in connection with vehicle repairs. (Examples include alternative transportation, towing costs.) _____

_____

Description of non-removable options that have been added to my vehicle after the sale, but not included in the vehicle purchase price. (Examples include sunroof, rustproofing, roof rack, pinstriping, etc.)_____

_____

Description of missing equipment or serious unrepaired vehicle damage. *(Do not include normal wear and tear such as minor dents, scratches, pitted glass, soiled carpets, minor stains or tears.)*_____

_____

I offer to return my vehicle and transfer title after the manufacturer meets my demand for Lemon Law relief.

Owner name ▓▓▓▓▓▓▓▓▓ Co-owner (if any)_____

Address ▓▓▓▓▓▓▓▓▓▓▓▓▓▓▓▓

Home phone (optional) ▓▓▓▓▓▓ Work phone (optional) ▓▓▓▓▓▓

Fax (optional)_____ Owner signature ▓▓▓▓▓▓

Double Standard Test Form (Page 2 of 2)

Vehicle repair information

I have made my vehicle available to an authorized dealership for repair because of the defect(s) on these dates:

Date in/out	Mileage	Dealership name	Problems you reported
11/5/01	9,684	Heiser Ford	STARTING PROBLEM— SOMETIMES WHEN TURNING KEY NOTHING HAPPENS. I THEN HAVE TO LET CAR SIT FOR AWHILE.
11/7/01 – 11/13/01	9,910	HEISER FORD	" "
7/12/02 – 7/17/02	27,578	HEISER FORD	" "
7/18/02 – 7/23/02	27,658	HEISER FORD	" "
7/26/02 – 8/2/02	27,838	HEISER FORD	" "

We recommend you send this notice to the manufacturer by certified mail.
Keep a copy for your records.

I AM ALSO SENDING COPIES OF PARERWORK FROM HEISER.

Double Standard Test: DAVIS/FORD

Date of Test:	August 2002
Proctor:	Vincent P. Megna
Consumer:	Mary Davis
	(Name changed to protect the innocent)
Manufacturer:	Ford Motor Company
Manufacturer's	
Representative:	Jimmy Pulaski
	(Name changed to protect myself)

Mary's 2001 black Focus had a starting problem. She had been stranded, towed, helped by strangers. She was better off popping the clutch to start the car than using the key. Ford tried repeatedly to correct the condition, but failed. Mary's case met all Lemon Law criteria. This would be an excellent test for Henry's Company. Let's see if this consumer gets what she is entitled to get. It hasn't happened in 13 years, but there is always a chance.

With a little help, Mary filled out the State-approved Motor Vehicle Lemon Law Notice and the Dispute Settlement Board application. Both were sent by certified mail, return receipt requested. **The Test** had begun.

Within one week, Jimmy Pulaski, a "gentleman" with Ford Motor Company, called Mary at work. Undoubtedly a Lemon Law technocrat, Mr. P. informed Mary that her Focus did not qualify under Wisconsin law. It had TOO MANY MILES, 31,000. Ford would not be able to provide a new car, but would give her the "coveted" Premium Care Package.

Thirteen years, one thousand cases, how could I miss the mileage limitation? It's downright embarrassing. And, all those corporate attorneys who never raised the "Pulaski Defense." It has to be embarrassing for them, too. Think of the cases manufacturers could have won.

Wait a minute. If no one has raised the mileage limitation in 13 years, maybe one doesn't exist. Maybe Mr. P. is wrong. Maybe he made a mistake. He might have THOUGHT there was a mileage limit. I'll bet that's it. Jimmy just made a simple mistake. It can happen to anybody. Still, he didn't test well.

Manufacturer's Test Result: F

We sued Ford and got nearly double the purchase price plus attorney fees.

Afterthought

I'm not after *The Guinness Book of World Records* for Most Consecutive Lemons. I may hold that one already. I'm not even bucking for the most Lemon Law cases won, although I wouldn't mind. What I really want is to see the average guy get a fair shake. I want the industry to stop screwing people just because it can. I also want the death penalty for Detroit's Double Standard. Until then, lemon owners are well advised to retain counsel.

Kangaroo Courts of Arbitration

It is the right of the accused to be tried by a legally constituted court, not by a kangaroo court.

— **Justice William O. Douglas**
United States Supreme Court
Williams v. United States, 1951

The concept of Kangaroo Court began in the pioneer days of 19th century America. Frontier judges took their own brand of "frontier justice" to rural people by traveling from town to town and conducting lightning fast trials. Often these roaming jurists were paid with fines they imposed. It was to their financial benefit to hear as many cases per day as daylight would allow. The more trials, the more convictions, the more money in their pockets. Law and justice were secondary concerns.

"Kangaroo Court" became American slang for unfair, biased, sham judicial proceedings. The term is commonly used to criticize courts and court decisions viewed to be unauthorized or irresponsible. In Kangaroo Court, the principles of law and justice are disregarded. In my opinion, much the same can be said of arbitration.

The process of arbitration dates back to the common law of England — the basis for our American jurisprudence. Under common law, arbitration comes about by agreement; arbitration can't be forced. Parties to a written contract voluntarily agree to submit disputes arising under the contract to arbitration. They give up their right to sue.

Contemporary arbitration is promoted as an informal process of dispute resolution. There are no judges. There are no juries. Arbitration is a substitute, if you will, for full-fledged litigation. Why go through all the time and expense of trial, when the matter can be taken care of outside the courtroom? My forefathers from the island of Sicily shared this viewpoint. They too had an informal process of dispute resolution.

I prefer the more formal approach to problem solving. I like rules. I like procedure. I like having a judge and jury hear my case BEFORE a decision is made. Call me silly, but that just seems to make more sense.

Webster's defines an arbitrator as "a person chosen to settle differences between two parties in controversy." Under this definition, Luca Brasi — the hit man from *The Godfather* — would make an excellent candidate. Who better to settle disputes than an overweight Italian with piano wire?

The word "arbitrator" comes from the word "arbitrary," meaning "at random and without reason," which clears up everything. Arbitrators render random decisions without reason because that's what they're supposed to do. That's why they're arbitrators. If they rendered well-reasoned legal decisions, they'd be judges.

Arbitration should have no place in Lemon Law. Yet, Lemon Law arbitration continues to run rampant. The auto industry successfully pitched arbitration as an inexpensive alternative to ugly civil litigation where only the lawyers get rich.

Almost all states require some form of arbitration within their Lemon Laws. They include manufacturer programs, state programs, certified programs, non-certified programs, programs that comply, programs that don't comply, qualified programs, unqualified programs, arbitration boards, arbitration panels, dispute settlement procedures, dispute settlement mechanisms, binding arbitration, non-binding arbitration. Wherever we turn with a car problem — the dealer, the manufacturer, the state, the warranty book — someone tells us to go to arbitration.

Think about this: Most consumers participating in arbitration are doing so for the first time. They have no experience in dispute resolution or law. Many don't even know the meaning of arbitration or alternative dispute resolution.

Legal novices are asked not only to participate in the arbitration process, but to also take the lead in presenting their cases. They are called upon to give opening statements and closing arguments, question and cross-examine witnesses, consider expert opinions and discuss legal principles. Formidable tasks for lawyers, they are EXTRAORDINARY tasks for electricians and daycare providers.

The Manufacturers' Programs

Most auto manufacturers have Kangaroo Court systems in place. For example, at last count 32 manufacturers, including General Motors, Honda, and Saab, use the Better Business Bureau AUTO LINE. The BBB is the largest Kangaroo operation in the country.

Ford has created its own system called the Dispute Settlement Board, handling only Ford disputes. In some states, DaimlerChrysler's Customer Arbitration Process funnels claims to the National Center for Dispute Settlement. This Kangaroo system located in Dallas, Texas, also arbitrates cases involving Toyota and a few other manufacturers.

These Kangaroo Courts, or "informal dispute settlement procedures," as Detroit would prefer them to be called, all have one thing in common: The consumer almost always loses.

Ford and the Dispute Settlement Board

The Dispute Settlement Board is Ford's "independent dispute settlement procedure." I like to think of it as Ford's private Kangaroo Court. Ford controls it. Ford funds it. Think of it as Ford's way of policing itself. And, we all know how well that works.

The DSB brochure tells us, "The Dispute Settlement Board is a voluntary, free, independent dispute-settlement program" that offers "an important benefit to you...." From personal experience, the only benefit I ever receive from the DSB is when they refuse to hear a case and I get to take it to court. The brochure goes on to tell us to see our dealer if we have a service or product complaint.

"We recommend that you attempt to resolve your concern with the Service Manager." If that doesn't work, see "the General Manager." If that doesn't work, call "Customer Assistance." Now we're getting someplace. If Customer Assistance can't take care of a problem, who can?

If you're still not satisfied after customer assistance, YOU are the problem, not your car. And, if you continue to complain, you get **The Board**.

I randomly pulled 27 decisions that my office received from the DSB over the last couple of years. I know consumers lose most of the time with Ford, but I wanted some hard stats. Out of the 27 cases, 20 were denial decisions and 7 ordered buybacks. That's 74.1 percent for the company, 25.9 percent for the consumer.

I'm actually surprised that Ford ruled against itself one out of four times. I guess that gives the impression of impartiality. According to *West's Encyclopedia of American Law*, that's better than the norm. *West's* finds less than 10 percent of the cases handled by a manufacturer-sponsored panel are decided in the consumer's favor. But I took a close look at the 20 Ford cases where the claims were denied. Here's what Ford's board found in those Twenty Denial Decisions:

The Board concluded that...

The vibration you reported is a normal operating characteristic for this type of vehicle.

The transmission, engine noise, no start, brakes and electrical system concerns you reported have been repaired.

The clutch, speedometer, sensor, engine noise and door alignment concerns you reported have been resolved.

The seat, engine and wiring system concerns you reported have been resolved.

The engine light, engine, electrical system and seat track concerns you reported have been resolved.

The transmission and vibration concerns you reported have been resolved.

The traction control was confirmed and the dealership will address this concern under the terms of your warranty.

The engine, oil consumption, cylinder leakage, gauges, cruise control, acceleration noise, and noise under the hood concerns you reported have been resolved.

The electrical system and surging concerns you reported could not be confirmed.

The related vibration, runs rough, rough idle, engine mounts and insulator concerns you reported have been resolved.

The brake concern you reported is a normal operating characteristic for this type of vehicle.

The paint concern you reported has been resolved.

The traction control and transmission concerns are normal operating characteristics for this type of vehicle.

The brake concern you reported is a normal operating characteristic for this type of vehicle.

The electrical system, power windows, interior lights, and water leak concerns you reported have been resolved.

The transmission, surging and loss of power concerns you reported have been resolved.

The acceleration noise and suspension concerns you reported could not be confirmed.

The compass, wipers, engine, oil leak, engine light, seat, molding, overhead console, and weather stripping concerns you reported have been resolved. The stalling and no start concerns you reported could not be confirmed.

Ford is to replace all four wheels and tires other than FIRESTONE. Your request for a refund or replacement is denied.

The significance of the Twenty Decisions is not that they went against the consumer. That is the norm. The significance is how wrong they were. Every one of the consumers who lost in the above decisions should have won. We proved that point by filling lawsuits against Ford in all 20 of the Denial Decisions. We settled every case, and not just for a few thousand dollars and some pocket change. Each one of the losers at Ford's Kangaroo Court received no less than a full refund on their vehicles. Some got more.

The DaimlerChrysler Customer Arbitration Process

The DaimlerChrysler Customer Arbitration Process has its own brochure handed out with new DaimlerChrysler vehicles in some states. As with Ford, we are told to try to resolve our problems with the dealer. If that doesn't work, call customer relations. And, if we're still not happy, the final step is arbitration.

The brochure goes on to say that the Customer Arbitration Process is offered to "ensure customer satisfaction." Being the owner of a Chrysler 300M, I certainly feel a lot better knowing that a procedure is in place to ensure my satisfaction. Page 3 of the brochure is also very reassuring. I am told, "There is no need to hire a lawyer to handle what could be costly and time-consuming legal action."

I am truly touched by Chrysler's genuine concern for my financial well-being. Why should I waste money on some scum-sucking, low-life, bottom-feeding lawyer when I don't need one? Thank you, DaimlerChrysler.

WARNING!
Be extremely concerned when your
multibillion-dollar adversary with 25,000
attorneys on retainer says, "YOU don't need
a lawyer to fight us. YOU can beat us yourself."

Law is not a do-it-yourselfer's playground. It's not like putting up a fence or plunging a toilet, although some might disagree on the latter. The field of law is complex, riddled with rules and regulations. It takes seven years — four in undergraduate, three in law school — to get a degree. Remember that $300 you lent your brother-in-law? Remember how hard it was to collect? It is a lot more difficult going up against one of the biggest corporations in the world. Believe me.

The National Center for Dispute Settlement

In my research for this chapter, the National Center for Dispute Settlement, NCDS, was by far the most helpful of the "independent" arbitration organizations. They provided me with 710 pages of audits for Toyota, Mitsubishi and DaimlerChrysler for the years 1999, 2000 and 2001. In contrast, the Better Business Bureau AUTO LINE managed to narrow its 67,624 cases filed between 2000 and 2002 down to 1 page. You gotta love that BBB.

Ford's Dispute Settlement Board also went all out for me. They wrote a one-page letter to Ken Press, the publisher of this book, stating that the DSB Administration Office "does not maintain statistical data specifically listing the number of denials, refund/replacements, or other decisions ordered by the Dispute Settlement Board." How convenient is that? However, I already know the results strongly favor Detroit. They always do.

Consider our friend, the National Center for Dispute Settlement. Of 4,160 Toyota cases that went to the NCDS in 1999, 2000 and 2001, only 764 (18.4 percent) resulted in favorable consumer decisions. Likewise, only 21.6 percent of the Mitsubishi cases heard in 2001 were in favor of the consumer. Surprisingly, Chrysler owners did much better at the NCDS. About 40 percent of the 8,000 DaimlerChrysler decisions in 2000 and 2001 were in favor of the consumer. It wouldn't surprise me to see Chrysler switch to the BBB.

State-Run Programs

Fourteen states run their own Lemon Law Kangaroo Courts. The question is WHY? Florida can't count votes in a presidential election, yet, they're going to tell me if I've got a lemon. In New Hampshire, it's all politics, with the Governor appointing the members who serve on the "court."

Georgia, another state running its own arbitration board, can't even decide on its own flag. They finally removed the Confederate battle emblem added back in 1956 as Georgia schools were being ordered to desegregate. They replaced it in 2003 with a redesigned flag resembling the Confederate "stars and bars" banner. What next? Stick people being hanged ala *South Park*? The states should get out of the "dispute settlement" business and go back to collecting sales tax and balancing their budgets.

Just because your state is involved with arbitration doesn't mean you get a break. You don't. I called the Vermont Motor Vehicle Arbitration Board to ask if I could have an attorney represent me at a state-run hearing. I was encouraged not to hire an attorney because the program was "very low-key."

I was told, "You know your case better than anyone. If you have an attorney, he can't testify." I had absolutely no idea what this person was trying to communicate. Of course, attorneys don't testify.

I asked whether the decisions were binding and how often consumers won. I was told that consumers get refunds or replacements about 50 percent of the time in Vermont (am I supposed to be impressed?) and that the Arbitration Board's decisions are final. I'm just happy none of my lemons came from Vermont.

Because many state arbitration decisions are BINDING, state programs can be even more damaging to consumers than manufacturer programs — which are usually not binding. If you lose in binding arbitration, it's over. The state of Connecticut gives an excellent warning about the finality of arbitration and the need for counsel in its May 2002 Automotive Dispute Settlement Program brochure:

> In most cases, the decision of the arbitrators will be final. You will not be able to appeal the decision to the court except under very limited circumstances. Therefore, if you are considering taking legal action against the manufacturer of your automobile, you should consult with a private attorney *BEFORE* signing the Agreement to Arbitrate.

Let's Talk Texas

Texas has a state run arbitration program. It also has a state-run execution program. The execution program is the most fatally efficient in the nation. The arbitration program sucks. Texas is very proud of both.

Every July, Texas publishes its Annual Lemon Law Report. This 50-page booklet tells its citizens what an outstanding job the Texas Motor Vehicle Board is doing for THEM. Texas is fighting Detroit on THEIR behalf. Texas is protecting THEM from complicated and expensive lawsuits. I can hear *The Yellow Rose of Texas* playing in my head. In reality, this report provides the evidence of the abysmal failure of Texas' state-run arbitration.

In 2001, 943 arbitration complaints were filed in Texas. With a few carrying over from the previous year, 953 were resolved. The Texas report claims that consumers received "some type of relief" 68.1 percent of the time. What exactly is "some type of relief?"

In Texas, "some type of relief" does not usually mean a refund or replacement. It means extended warranties, repairs, trade-assists and other types of "goodwill" tokens. So, if KIA gives you four car payments or GM settles for that extended warranty, you're a winner in Texas. You're in the 68th percentile.

Of the 953 cases filed in Texas in 2001, only 244 consumers (25.6 percent) received a repurchase or replacement. Another 402 got next to nothing — those trade-assists, extended warranties, repairs or other relief. And 307 got nothing at all.

Of the 953 cases, 795 were resolved without a hearing. Only 158 arbitration hearings actually took place. Those Texan arbitrators sure work their butts off. And of those 158 hearings, the consumer received a repurchase or replacement only 39 times.

The booklet goes on to state that manufacturers "view the Lemon Law as an opportunity to improve customer satisfaction and increase market share instead of costly litigation where success is defined as winning at any cost." Of course, it's an opportunity. It's an opportunity for the manufacturer to screw the consumer 75 percent of the time. Detroit loves Texas.

Let's put this in perspective. Texas is the second largest state in the union. It has a population of 22 million. The Texas Motor Vehicle Board has nine members. The Texas Department of Transportation Consumer Affairs Section has 15 employees.

That gives Texas 24 government positions to handle Lemon Law cases.

In comparison, the population of Waukesha, Wisconsin, (where my office is located) is 65,000. We have three attorneys, one paralegal and one secretary handling Lemon Law cases. In 2001, through the efforts of my firm, Jastroch & LaBarge, S.C., Detroit repurchased — not necessarily voluntarily — about 150 vehicles. Not as many as Texas with 244, but we're not *quite* as big as Texas.

Defense Counsel

Last year, at the International Association of Lemon Law Administrators (IALLA) Conference in Orlando (Disney World is my favorite place), I spoke with an auto industry defense attorney from New York. We met at the welcoming reception. The truth does have a way of coming out over free beer and cheese.

This "so proud to defend Detroit" shark told me that his firm specialized in representing Chrysler and other manufacturers at state-run Lemon Law arbitration hearings. They were currently in three states but wanted to go nationwide. His firm went after the "little guy" in arbitration with reckless abandon.

I asked my new drinking buddy how often the "little guy" had an attorney back East. "Not too often," he replied. "We've got 'em trained, but it doesn't matter. Consumers do worse when they show up with lawyers. They lose the sympathy of the arbitrator. And their lawyers aren't very good anyway."

There you have it. Arbitration has all the elements of a no-win situation. If you go it alone, you're going to get screwed, but with sympathy. If you take a lawyer, you're going to get screwed without sympathy. I think it's time for divine intervention.

The Prayer

Consumers don't have a prayer at arbitration. That's why I wrote one. To be most effective, the prayer should be memorized and recited with feeling. You may kneel or remain upright. I have found that some arbitrators are more sympathetic to kneeling. Others prefer that the consumer stand reverently with head slightly bowed. In either case, be sincere. The arbitrator can spot a phony. Show the arbiter due respect. And, don't be afraid to choke up, or shed a tear during the recitation. Good luck.

The Consumer's Prayer at Arbitration

Oh Most Holy Arbiter on high. Oh Merciful One. Most Gracious One! I come before you in time of great need. Thee with infinite wisdom and humble understanding, who presides over this most sacred of all Mechanisms, encouraged by Congress and created by the Mighty Philistine. I am not worthy to stand in your presence, to seek compassion, to beg for your mercy. I am a vassal in your midst, oh Hallowed Arbiter, Exalted Sage.

With guidance from the Almighty Industry, I have overcome the fear of confrontation and have initiated resolution through the Great Mechanism. I seek peace with the all-powerful Philistine and bow my head before You, my unbiased, impartial Ruler of Rulers.

In the name of Arbitration, I submit myself to Your Judgment and accept Your Word as THE WORD, Your Decision, as FINAL. I kneel before You, my anointed Judge AND Jury, seeking only justice and mercy. I pray, JUST THIS ONE TIME, that You consider both sides of the controversy, not just the side of Your Creator, the Goliath of Detroit. I ask you to disregard the long established prejudice within the Mechanism that so strongly favors the Giant and instead, turn to the revelation of the hallowed American prophet, Mr. Spike Lee, and Do the Right Thing.

I ask this in Your Name, Most Holy Arbiter, Most Gracious One. Thy Will be done, at arbitration as it is in Dearborn. In the name of Ford, General Motors and Chrysler. Ah Men.

You, Me and the BBB

> To guarantee impartiality,
> funding... is committed in
> advance by the participating
> companies.

> — **BBB AUTO LINE Brochure**
> February 2002

We've all heard of the Better Business Bureau. What exactly they do, I'm not sure. They claim to be a corporation organized by businesses to protect the public — a pretty large segment of society — from unfair advertising and business practices. They have offices in more than 200 cities in the United States. The Ku Klux Klan also claims to protect me. They fight for my rights as an oppressed white man in America. The Klan has about 6,000 members living primarily in the South. I am touched by such benevolent entities looking out for my best interest, but I can take care of myself.

I don't need private corporations or white hooded people thinking of ways to protect me. I'll do just fine without the BBB, and far better without the KKK! However, my purpose is not to rip the Better Business Bureau in general. I'd like to be more specific.

The BBB AUTO LINE handles about 25,000 claims per year involving automotive disputes. Operating in every state, AUTO LINE is the largest of the so-called "informal dispute settlement procedures." The 32 auto manufacturers that participate in the BBB program also pay for the program. I don't like that idea. I don't want the entity hearing my claim to be paid by the entity I'm going after. I don't care how impartial they claim to be. Detroit money keeps the BBB AUTO LINE in business. And that's a conflict in my book. And this IS my book!

How It Works

A consumer with a defective vehicle who has talked to the service manager, talked to the general manager, called customer assistance, but still can't get anywhere, calls BBB AUTO LINE in Arlington, Virginia. A case specialist takes information over the phone. A package of materials is mailed to the complaining consumer. The package contains a Claim Form, Agreement to Arbitrate, Program Summary, Standards of the Lemon Law, Remedies of the Lemon Law and a 28-page booklet that includes the Rules of Arbitration.

The consumer, who has yet to budge the manufacturer one inch, now has fifty pages of confusing mumbo-jumbo in her possession. She is instructed to review the information in preparation for taking on her personal Giant at a hearing.

The BBB booklet tells you how to prepare your case and what will happen at the hearing. I can tell you what will happen. You'll lose — most of the time. According to *West's Encyclopedia of American Law*, consumers win a little more than 10 percent of the time in BBB AUTO LINE. My personal experience with AUTO LINE is about the same as with Ford's Dispute Settlement Board — 25 percent in favor of the consumer, 75 percent against.

Here's what the 2002 booklet tells you about your hearing:

"You should be prepared to convince the arbitrator your position is right." *Yes, that is the reason I am here.*

"Present documents and witnesses in support of your case." *Thank you. I had originally planned to call witnesses in support of GM's case.*

"Question witnesses who testify on behalf of the company." *Wait a second. Isn't this cross-examination? I better do some research at the nearest law library.*

"Rebut any testimony or evidence presented by the company." *Easier said than done. Law schools offer courses on rebuttal. I will try to enroll before the hearing.*

"All parties will be given an opportunity to review and comment on the findings and credentials of technical experts." *Great, I can't even change my own oil but I'll be ready to critique the résumé of some engineering powertrain expert.*

After the case has been presented, "… be prepared to give a summary of your position, deal with any questions that have not been answered and tell the arbitrator what you think the decision should be and why." *Isn't this a closing argument? While I'm taking Rebuttal at law school, I'll audit a course on Trial Techniques.*

Stay "… within the bounds of common courtesy and conventional language." *This means I can't tell the arbitrator to go fuck himself.*

And how long should this legal affair take? ONE HOUR! That's right, the BBB says we should restrict "presentation to NO MORE THAN ONE HOUR." They must know something I don't know.

In one recent case, not an overly complicated one, my office clocked 469 hours of attorney's time. We won, but it took 468 hours longer than the BBB thinks is sufficient for a consumer untrained in Lemon Law.

The BBB booklet goes on to list 29 AUTO LINE Arbitration Rules. These rules deal with the hearing, arbitrators, notice, media, attendance, evidence, procedure, experts, and the decision. Six pages alone are devoted to the decision, including modification, clarification, suspension, acceptance, rejection, reconsideration. Does the average consumer have a clue as to what all this means? I know lawyers who would be hard pressed to explain these rules. One in particular bears mentioning, Rule 25 J:

Verification of Performance

If the consumer accepts the decision, all parties must do what the decision requires within the time limits set by the arbitrator.

This sounds simple enough. If the consumer wins (and it does happen), the manufacturer must do what the arbitrator says. If he says, "Give the guy a new car," you'd think GM would just give the guy his new car. **But Noooo**. Sometimes, even when you win, you lose.

Kiss vs. General Motors

Peter Kiss was in the towing business. He purchased a new GMC Sierra 3500 tow truck from a local GMC dealer. A tow truck comes in two parts: cab and chassis, and the towing package. General Motors manufactured Peter's cab and chassis. Vulcan manufactured his towing package. The dealer put the truck together, attaching the Vulcan 882 towing package to the GMC Sierra 3500 cab and chassis. Peter paid $43,000 for his new tow truck.

During the first nine months of operation, the truck was towed more than it towed. Twenty-three separate problems plagued Peter. The brakes failed. The engine died. The transmission leaked. The shocks, the alternator, the headlights, all were defective. Peter's new tow truck was a lemon. He called the BBB AUTO LINE, GM's certified arbitration program in Wisconsin.

Peter's case was so clear that even the arbitrator agreed he had a lemon. A decision came down ordering GM to provide a "new motor vehicle substantially IDENTICAL to the replaced vehicle." Peter won. He beat his Giant. He beat GM. A new truck was on the way. Or was it?

A few months later, GM called. The truck was in and it was a beauty. All Peter had to do was drop off the "lemon" so the dealer could transfer the old Vulcan tow package to his new cab and chassis. Hold it. That wasn't the deal. No one ever said the old tow package was going to be transferred. Peter was awarded a "substantially identical" new vehicle, not half of one. The BBB decision was clear. New is new. Identical means identical.

Peter would not let his new tow truck be Frankensteined. It would not be put together with old parts. Peter fought GM for months, but GM wouldn't budge. There would be no new tow package. Period! Peter called my office for help.

This is an amazing business. A consumer finally gets a favorable decision and the manufacturer won't follow it. The arbitration decision required a new tow truck — cab, chassis AND towing package. That's what Peter bought. He didn't buy a used tow package on a new cab and chassis. If GM were allowed to get away with this, what would stop them from transferring tires, radios or even engines on other decisions requiring replacement vehicles? We filed suit against General Motors on November 16, 1998. I ended up arguing the case in the Wisconsin Court of Appeals. On May 9, 2001, the Court ruled in favor of Peter Kiss.

Now it was too late for GM to give Peter a new towing package. They had violated the Lemon Law. With Wisconsin's provision for double damages, we settled the case on August 8, 2001 for $96,000, plus attorney fees. From his initial call to the BBB, it had taken Peter three years and three hundred and three days to have his tow truck problem resolved.

The BBB and Me

I've tried to become a BBB arbitrator. I thought as long as we're stuck with this ridiculous arbitration sickness, I could help improve it. I could give something back.

The BBB publication clearly states: "AUTO LINE arbitrators are persons from your community who are interested in the fair resolution of consumer disputes." That's me. I'm from the neighborhood and I want consumers treated fairly. I'm against Kangaroo Courts, and the BBB desperately needs good arbitrators. So, I applied.

Annette Lee, the Arbitrator Recruitment Coordinator, responded in writing. She thanked me for my application and interest in the BBB AUTO LINE. My application had been carefully reviewed. It seems I "possess the key qualifications to participate in the BBB's AUTO LINE program." I can't wait to add this to my résumé. There was a slight catch. Because of my "experience," there was a "conflict of interest." They turned me down.

I wrote back. I told them that under the Rules of Professional Conduct and common law, I had no conflict of interest. Just because I represent consumers, doesn't mean I won't follow the law. It doesn't mean I won't be fair. It doesn't mean I am incapable of rendering impartial decisions. A conflict would only arise if one of MY clients were a party to the arbitration. Then, of course, I would step down. I asked the BBB to reconsider its decision.

Ms. Lee faxed me a letter saying that my application was "being re-reviewed by our legal staff," and I would hear from them shortly. I'm still waiting.

Here's the deal with the BBB. They don't want someone who knows the law making legal decisions. That could be dangerous. That would go against tradition. BBB arbitrators know little or nothing about Lemon Law. They are rarely lawyers and have no technical expertise.

BBB arbitrator training consists of a videotape, a home study manual and 13 hours of in-person sessions. Not quite the equivalent of a degree from Palo Alto. Nevertheless, these ersatz judges — about as qualified as parent referees at U-8 soccer games — are then certified to decide whether my Chevy Malibu is a lemon. They have something else in common with parent referees: BBB arbitrators don't get paid. They volunteer.

Frankly, I don't want some volunteer dentist hearing my case. Dentists don't know anything about Lemon Law. They fix teeth. Even with a videotape and 13 hours of training, my dentist wouldn't let me pull one of his central incisors. Why would I want him deciding whether or not my Corvette qualifies as a lemon? I don't want him playing lawyer, judge and jury in an arena where he doesn't belong. If my dentist wants to give something back to the community, he can clean my teeth for free.

And while we're at it, why do BBB arbitrators work for free? Why aren't they paid? The woman who sent me the fax gets paid. The legal staff gets paid. Other people who work for the BBB get paid. But AUTO LINE arbitrators volunteer their time. Why?

It makes no sense. We are dealing with the richest, most powerful corporations in the world. Even a referee at a college basketball game gets $750. But an arbitrator who decides whether GM takes back a $45,000 Cadillac gets nothing. Hasn't anyone ever heard, "You get what you pay for?"

Don't get me wrong. I'm all in favor of volunteer work. I salute the volunteers at nursing homes, VA hospitals and homeless shelters who give of their time and talents to help people in need. We all should seriously consider if we are doing enough in this area.

I do question, for example, why PGA tour events are staffed by volunteers. If golfers make millions (average purse for a tour event in 2003 was $4.7 million and a 20 ounce Pepsi costs $4), why doesn't the guy cooking hot dogs get paid? If I didn't have to pay my legal assistant, receptionist, or bookkeeper, I'd make a lot more money too. Better yet, if I could get a couple of lawyers to work for nothing, that would really put me on Easy Street. Frankly, I haven't been able to find good help willing to volunteer their time so that I can make more money. And I am not a good golfer. But back to the BBB.

What if Lemon Law arbitrators actually understood the Law? What if consumers started winning four out of five times or seven out of ten? GM and the other manufacturers might stop using the BBB AUTO LINE. The AUTO LINE could go out of business. The Better Business Bureau wouldn't like that.

The REAL problem with BBB arbitration is that consumers usually quit if they lose. They give up. When the Denial Decision arrives in the mail, Joe throws in the towel. He had his day in court and lost. If this arbitrator ruled against him, why would it be any different the next time around? The arbitrator knows what he's doing. Right? What the average Joe doesn't realize is that this decision came from a Kangaroo Court, and that means, it ain't over till it's over, Joe. You can still get justice.

I have represented hundreds of consumers who have lost at BBB arbitration hearings. Not one of those consumers who lost at the BBB ever lost in court. NOT ONE. Every BBB loser became a Lemon Law winner. All it took was filing a lawsuit.

Is this an endorsement of litigation? Is this the "sue the bastard" mentality? You bet it is. Do you have to go to court to get Lemon Law justice? You bet you do. The record speaks for itself. If you want what you're entitled to, if you want a fair shake, go to court, not the BBB. At the very least, go to court after the BBB. That's why we have courts. That's why we have judges. That's why we have a Seventh Amendment. You can get justice from a judge and jury. You seldom get justice from some unpaid, inexperienced, untrained, though well-meaning, volunteer.

The Seventh Amendment

In suits at common law, where the value in controversy shall exceed twenty dollars, **the right of a trial by jury shall be preserved**, and no fact tried by a jury, shall be otherwise re-examined in any Court of the United States, than according to the rules of the common law.

Trials and Tribulations

The first thing we do, let's kill all
the lawyers.

> — **William Shakespeare**
> *Henry VI*

Four hundred years ago, one of Shakespeare's characters suggested slaughtering all lawyers to make the world a better place. Today, many people still agree. I personally think that's a little harsh. However, I too am somewhat persuaded to the Shakespearean viewpoint every time I turn to the "Attorneys" section of the Yellow Pages. I hate to see my brothers and sisters of the bar begging.

State bar associations desperately want to change the lawyer image. They're sick of the lawyer jokes. They're tired of Jay Leno and Danny DeVito one-liners. They want respect. Following in the footsteps of automotive advertising gems like **"Zero Worries! That'll Be the Daewoo,"** the State Bar of Wisconsin has developed a slogan for its lawyers:

WISCONSIN LAWYERS
EXPERT ADVISERS. SERVING YOU.

They want us to affix this catchphrase to our letterheads, client communications and brochures. As if that weren't bad enough, we are told to take out professional image ads that read:

We are

your Little League coaches,
volunteer firefighters,
community leaders...

GIVE ME A BREAK. We are lawyers! It doesn't matter what
the public thinks of us. We're not in a popularity contest. I don't
deserve community recognition because I have a law degree and
decided to coach fifth-grade basketball. Why are we begging for
respect? Who cares? No one likes us. Get over it!

My job is representing my client's interest to the best of my
ability. End of story! That's why I get paid. That's why I went to
law school. Mother Theresa was respected. We're advocates. We
fight. We defend murderers, rapists, Jeffrey Dahmer. The public
isn't going to genuflect every time an attorney walks by, just
because we tell them we are godly members of the community.
Why should they? WE ARE LAWYERS.

I've handled over 1,000 automobile warranty claims. I live
and breathe Lemon Law. I feel the plaintiff's pain. I feel the plaintiff's frustration. I see only the plaintiff's side. In my mind,
Detroit can't win. Detroit has no defense to any of my cases and
how dare they think otherwise. We will prevail in settlement, at
trial or on appeal. That's what I think, believe, know.

I cringe when attorneys say, "You can win OR lose any
case." This isn't the NBA. A .500 record shouldn't be your goal in
law. We're not trying to make the playoffs. We're trying to beat
the Giant. That's why I show up at work every day, to fight.

Most cases settle out of court, either before filing a lawsuit
or after filing, but before trial. Only 2 percent of my cases go to
trial. This means that 98 out of 100 consumers receive a refund
or replacement vehicle without setting foot in a courtroom. This
is good news for the average guy because courtrooms are fright-
ening places. They are filled with uncertainty, surprise and
lawyers.

The Trial

Just so you'll know, it takes about a year and a half from the day a client walks into my office till the day I stand in front of a jury and give an opening statement. That might sound like a long time, but it isn't. A trial is complex, with many components and participants. Eighteen months to get a case tried is really quite good. For example, in Cook County, Illinois, it takes almost three years to bring a civil case to trial. And the Illinois Lemon Law already sucks. The auto manufacturer's lobby owns the Land of Lincoln.

While we wait for the trial date, a lot happens. Both sides do discovery. We get copies of their documents. They get copies of our documents. We take depositions. They take depositions. Our mechanical experts look at the vehicle. Their mechanical experts look at the vehicle. Our experts always find a problem because there is a problem. Their experts never find a problem because they are *their* experts.

In 13 years, only one engineer from Detroit has ever found a problem with any of my client's vehicles. Only one defense "hired gun" has ever found anything wrong. With all their engineering sophistication, these experts can't tell when a car won't start, when the brake pedal goes to the floor or when the sunroof leaks. It's incredible.

A typical Lemon Law trial takes about three days from beginning to end. Day one includes jury selection, opening statements and the start of testimony. The opening statement and closing argument are my favorite parts of the trial. This is the only time when I get to talk to the jury. The opening and closing are why I try cases. Everything else is so formal, so cold: Question, answer, question, objection, question, sustained, overruled, sidebar. I'd like to show up just at the beginning and the end of trial, but that wouldn't be polite.

The second day is boring. More testimony about work orders and repair visits, witnesses talking about engines, brakes, paint, etc. By this point, at LEAST two jurors have fallen asleep and have either been elbowed by a fellow juror or awakened by the judge. A more serious problem arises in trials without a jury when the judge starts nodding off. But that's another story.

On day three, the testimony is finally wrapped up, closing arguments are given and the jurors retire to deliberate. If all goes well, in a couple of hours, the jury returns with a plaintiff's verdict: "**The vehicle is a lemon.**"

At this point, I do a clenched fist power salute, pack up my stuff and return to the office. There, I scream at the top of my lungs and make an obscene gesture at the photo of Attorney James A. Brown. The trial is over.

The Judge

Judges referee, just like at a football game. They control the trial, interpret law, rule on evidence and insure fairness. No two judges are alike. Every judge runs his or her courtroom differently. The law remains the same, but is treated differently from court to court.

Gerry Spence, the great plaintiff's counsel from Jackson, Wyoming, is no fan of the bench. In his book *O. J. The Last Word*, Attorney Spence is quite pronounced in his feelings for those we call "Your Honor." Blockheads in robes, despots, mammal-eating monsters spewing venom randomly over the courtroom, tyrants pacing back and forth across their little stage, smirking, peering down, hollering, interrupting, and intimidating are but some of the descriptives used by Mr. Spence when discussing these public servants.

All things considered, I get along pretty well with the judiciary. Maybe it's because I play in the band Presumed Guilty with three of Wisconsin's finest judges. Or maybe it's because Wisconsin is a pro-consumer state where judges understand how difficult it is for "David" to go against Detroit. In some states, it is left to the discretion of the judges whether to award attorney fees in Lemon Law litigation. Without judicial understanding that attorneys must be paid if they win, the Lemon Law fails. As I've said before and may well say again, if lawyers don't get paid for taking on Detroit and winning, no lawyer will take on Detroit.

The Jury

The jury represents the power of the people, the voice of common sense, the great equalizer and the collective wisdom of the community. The jury is pure, untainted and unblemished by the technicalities of law. The jury is apolitical and nongovernmental with the unemployed sheet metal worker, the checkout clerk, the homemaker and the accountant all working together towards the common goal of truth. The jury sees through phony attorneys, fake sincerity and corporate bullshit. The jury is the soul of the trial. I believe in the jury.

I remember one Ford lawyer telling the jury during her opening statement, "I am honored to represent Ford Motor Company." Meanwhile, I'm thinking, "Apparently, you've never heard of the Pinto or the Crown Victoria's current problem of exploding in rear-end crashes. You do corporate defense work. You'll represent any company, anywhere, for any reason, as long as there is a retainer. And the jury knows that too."

The Facts

I try to know every fact of my case, and Lemon Law cases are usually fact-intense. One simple fact can change the entire outcome. Consider the case of Dave and Carol D.

Dave and Carol D. filed a lemon lawsuit against Ford. Their Mercury Tracer had a transmission problem. Sometimes it would hesitate between first and second gear, and second and third gear. The transmission seemed to go into neutral causing the car to lose five or six miles per hour during those seconds of transmission delay. My clients were concerned about safety. A tailgater could hit them from behind when the car temporarily lost speed.

Early on in the case, I spoke to a potential witness — my clients' 15-year-old daughter. She was aware of the problem and would make an excellent witness. Ford deposed Mr. and Mrs. D., but not their daughter. Ford wanted to keep costs down. That was a big mistake on their part.

About two weeks before trial, we began intense preparation. My clients' daughter was now almost 16 years old. She'd had her temporary license for several months and was learning to drive. The problem, a very serious one, became clear. She was learning in the Mercury Tracer. Our potential deathtrap had been turned into a driver's ed vehicle for a high school sophomore by her parents. If this fact came out at trial, we could very well lose. The jury might not see my clients' concern over safety as valid.

I didn't call the daughter to the stand. Ford could have. They didn't. I didn't ask Dave or Carol about how the Tracer was currently being used. Ford could have. They didn't. Ford never discovered the fact that could have cost us the case. The jury returned a plaintiff's verdict.

The parents weren't thinking, true, but the car was still unsafe. That was the point of our case that did not change with the parents' actions. Ford had as much access to the information as I had. I looked for that one important case-changing fact. They, on the other hand, missed it completely.

The Sins of the Son

I've sued General Motors — the largest auto manufacturer in the world — 350 times. My office has never lost, not one case, not one motion. In 13 years, GM has never beaten one of my clients. GM's only trial court victory against one of my clients was reversed on appeal.

General Motors paid for my 2002 Corvette and bought back my 1997 Cadillac. They continue to pay me $225 an hour to sue them. That's about $75 an hour more than they pay their own attorneys. You'd think they would look at me as a member — a stepchild of sorts — of their corporate family.

I like General Motors. My first car was a 1958 Chevrolet Impala. Fifteen of my nineteen automobiles were manufactured by GM. I buy American. You won't find a Toyota or Honda in my garage. Connie owned a Corvair. My son drives a Camaro. And my dad is currently on his tenth Caddy. As Hank Williams, Jr. would say: *"It's a Family Tradition."*

I generally like the way General Motors treats my clients. GM is more compassionate than the other manufacturers. I'm not saying they have a heart; I wouldn't go that far. But General Motors is less warlike than the rest of the industry. I like their lawyers. I like their paralegals. I like their approach to claim resolution once they've been sued. That's why I was a little surprised when GM reminded me that they were still Goliath. They went after my father.

In 1965, my father, Vincent R. Megna, bought his first Cadillac, a used 1961 Coupe DeVille. He was 43 years old. Owning a Caddy had been his dream since the day he got his driver's license. The name Cadillac meant something thirty, forty years ago. Cadillac was the flagship of the industry, the car by which all others were judged. Beginning in 1915 with an ad in the *Saturday Evening Post*, Cadillac hailed itself as a "Standard for the World." Luxury, style, prestige, Cadillac had everything. Even today when there are any number of high-end, luxury vehicles on the road, Cadillac remains a premium quality motorcar for the discriminating buyer. My father bought nine more Cadillacs after the '61 Coupe. Only one gave him trouble.

His 1997 Sedan DeVille had a starting problem. The engine didn't always turn over on the first try. It would crank but not start. At times it took two, three or even four attempts to get running. This condition happened about ten separate times during a three-year period. This '97 certainly wasn't the "Standard for the World" that Cadillac promised.

Cadillacs SHOULD start when the key is turned. All vehicles should, even those KIAs. If they don't, dealers should fix them. In this case, the dealers could never duplicate the problem. They'd say, "Bring it back when it's happening. Bring it back when it acts up." But it was happening. It was acting up. That's why the car was in the shop. Why not just fix it? I've never liked the runaround, given to me or anyone else. It was time to take a professional look at the situation.

Now, my father has never sued anyone. I've done enough suing for the whole family. But he did have a problem. His car didn't start right and the dealer couldn't or wouldn't fix it. If this case walked into my office, I'd take it in a heartbeat. This was a good Magnuson-Moss case — the dealer failed to repair a malfunction within a reasonable time. The starting problem had been going on for three years, including eleven visits to the shop. I sent a notice to GM.

Greg Garguilo at the General Motors Business Resource Center responded in writing with a $1,000 offer. That's very gracious, Greg, but I don't like being slapped around. By the way, whatever happened to the industry's double standard where the lawyer gets preferential treatment? This was starting to look personal. GM was going to make my father pay for the sins of his son.

Vincent R. Megna, Sr. v. General Motors Corporation and Crest Cadillac was filed on July 10, 2001. GM's defense was that I, the Lemon Law lawyer, had set up this whole thing. There was no case. There was no defect. GM contended that I thought they would settle, that I encouraged my father to take his car in and then directed his every move. I was working the system. I was taking advantage of the largest auto manufacturer in the world.

The following testimony was taken from the deposition of Mary C. Bristow, the GM spokesperson and representative. For purposes of this case, Ms. Bristow WAS General Motors. The deposition was taken on April 3, 2002:

Q. *Do you have any reason to believe that Mr. Megna did not have starting problems with his vehicle?*

A. Personally I wonder, yes.

Q. *Why?*

A. The nature of his relationship with his son, what his son does for a living. Those would be the things I'd have concern with.

Q. *And why does his relationship with his son concern you?*

A. … he's very familiar with the manner in which General Motors tries to address these types of issues with regard to Lemon Law or Magnuson-Moss claims.

Q. *And if I understand you correctly, you believe that the fact that the plaintiff, Mr. Megna's son, is an attorney, that for some reason you question the validity of Mr. Megna, the plaintiff's, complaints regarding his vehicle?*

A. I have concerns about that.

Q. *So you don't believe that there's any merit to the plaintiff's claim in this case?*

A. … I don't believe it's a valid request.

There was one major flaw in GM's argument. IT WASN'T TRUE. I didn't encourage my father to file a claim. I wasn't working the system. The Cadillac had a problem — a starting problem. In their zeal, GM never objectively looked at the claim. They didn't see the problem with the car. They saw only me.

Our case was straightforward. The dealer, Crest Cadillac, never took the time to find out what was wrong with the car. The starting condition could have been easily repaired. In fact, another Cadillac dealer did repair the car three months *after* the warranty expired. That dealer found the defect in 30 minutes. That dealer charged my father $196 and the starting problem never came back.

The trial lasted three days. The jury deliberated four hours. They found that the starting problem was not repaired within a reasonable time. GM and Crest Cadillac lost. The verdict was $10,000 against General Motors and $196 against Crest. Since this was a Mag-Moss case, we asked the court to award the sum of $114,000 in attorney fees and costs. My firm had put in 469 hours to solve a problem that could have been initially handled by a mechanic in 30 minutes, at a cost of less than $200.

GM now argued that we spent too much time on the case and only deserved $10,000 in fees. However, during the battle over fees, GM's attorneys, Bowman and Brooke, were required to provide a statement of THEIR time spent on the case. Astonishingly, they had logged an incredible 809 hours trying to beat the Megnas! I was truly honored by this commitment of time and resources to my father's case, almost twice the time my firm had expended. Quite a compliment.

The Court was equally impressed. It awarded us every cent in attorney fees and costs that we requested.

General Motors, one of the most powerful corporations in the world, came to Waukesha, Wisconsin, to prove a point. I don't know exactly what that point might have been, but I'm

GM Offer Letter for Vincent Megna, Sr. (Page 1 of 2)

GENERAL MOTORS BUSINESS RESOURCE CENTER

May 10, 2001

VIA FAX ONLY

Vincent P. Megna, Esq.
Jastroch and LaBarge, S.C.
640 West Moreland Blvd.
Waukesha, Wisconsin 53187

Re: Vincent Robert Megna, Sr. v. General Motors Corporation
       1997 Cadillac Deville
       VIN #

Dear Mr. Megna.:

We regret that your client is dissatisfied with his 1997 Cadillac Deville and that several attempts by the dealer to resolve his concerns have not met his expectations. General Motors takes great pride in the service we provide to our customers, and we apologize for any inconvenience and frustration he has experienced.

After careful research and evaluation of the above case by General Motors Corporation, our research indicates the following facts:

◆   Within the first year of operation, your client's vehicle was out of service by reason of warranty repair for 5 days.
◆   A non-conformity causing the brake fluid level to be improperly reported to the driver information center was repaired during the first reported service visit of August 17, 1997. As there have been no further reports alleging manufacturing defect with regard the brake fluid level in 44 months and 29,000 miles of operation that followed, we must conclude that the defect does not continue to exist.
◆   The vehicle was presented for non-conformities in the front and rear bumper inserts on October 7, 1997. Repairs conducted during the first service opportunity returned the vehicle to operation within manufacturer specifications. As the concern has not been again reported to any authorized General Motors service facility in the subsequent 43 months and 28,000 miles of vehicle operation, we must conclude that the non-conformity does not continue to exist.
◆   Performance of a safety campaign on November 18, 1997 resulted in a single day out of service.
◆   On January 9, 1998, the vehicle was presented with a concern in the operation of the left side windshield washer. The dealership found a plugged washer nozzle, which was promptly corrected. Again, there have been no further reports of non-conformities in the vehicle's windshield washer system in over 39 months of subsequent operation. We conclude that the prior non-conformity does not continue to exist.
◆   The vehicle was presented for repairs on February 25, 1998 reporting a concern of "car stalling out when start and then hard to restart". The dealership diagnosed and corrected the non-conformity in the gear indicator system. The non-conformity corrected on this occasion is not related to the service to de-carbon the throttle body plates 12 months later, or the failed battery diagnosed in November of 2000.
◆   No non-conformity in vehicle operation has been the subject of four or more unsuccessful repair opportunities during the term of the New Vehicle Limited Warranty.

After careful review of this case, Cadillac Division of General Motors would like to make the following voluntary offer of an Owner Loyalty Certificate as settlement for all defendants. This offer is being made in an effort to reach an early resolution that will be equitable to your client and reinforce General Motors' commitment to its customers.

General Motors Corp. – CARS – Legal, c/o MSX International, MC 336-105-000
1464 John A. Papalas Drive, Lincoln Park, MI 48146-1460

GM Offer Letter for Vincent Megna, Sr. (Page 2 of 2)

May 10, 2001
Page 2

- ◆ $1,000.00 Owner Loyalty Certificate, good for the period of 1 year from the date of issuance, when applied toward the purchase or lease of a new Cadillac vehicle.

General Motors Corporation will continue to assist you in addressing any outstanding concerns in accordance with the terms of the existing warranty coverages. If this offer is acceptable to your client, please have your client sign this offer letter as well as the attached release and return them to me via fax or mail. Once I receive the signed acceptance and release, your client will receive the settlement by mail within 15 business days.

If you have any questions or need further clarification, please feel free to contact me at the number listed below.

Very truly yours,

Greg Gargullo
BRC Legal Case Manager
Ph# 800-231-1841, prompt 9, extension 58704
FAX# 1-813-635-4081

cc: FILE

Attach.

_____
Signature

_____
Date

General Motors Corp. – CARS – Legal, c/o MSX International, MC 336-105-000
1464 John A. Papalas Drive, Lincoln Park, MI 48146-1460

Attachment to GM Offer Letter for Vincent Megna, Sr.

RELEASE OF CLAIM

I, Vincent R Megna, Sr, in consideration of a $1,000.00 Cadillac Owner Loyalty Certificate provided by General Motors Corporation, hereby release and discharge General Motors Corporation, its authorized independent dealers, designers and suppliers of vehicles, parts and components that are distributed by General Motors Corporation, and their respective agents and employees from any and all claims and causes of action for any injuries, losses or damages to my person and/or property which may have been caused by, or which may at any time arise out of, or in connection with one __1997 Cadillac DeVille__ bearing Vehicle Identification Number ▮▮▮▮▮▮▮▮▮▮.

The mileage was _____ on _____ , the date of the signing of this release.

The undersigned has carefully read and understands this release and signs it to resolve the claim described above.

DATE SIGNED: _____

_____
Claimant

_____
Address

_____
City, State, Zip Code

_____
Social Security Number

In the STATE OF _____ , COUNTY OF _____ ss.
The foregoing instrument was acknowledged before me this _____ (date)
by _____who is personally known to me or
who has produced _____(type of identification) as
identification. The foregoing instrument was executed the same as his free act and deed.

Notary Public _____

_____ County

Cost of the Megna Trial

Total amount awarded to Megna, Sr.	$10,196
Court costs	$6,485
Plaintiff's attorney fees (Megna, Jr. and associates)	$108,502
GM defense attorney fees (reported)	$82,462*
Interest paid by GM on plaintiff's attorney fees	$2,000

Total amount paid by GM	**$209,645**

*Only includes GM attorney fees paid through the Megna trial.
 GM did not report what it paid in additional attorney fees for
 contesting the plaintiff's fee request.

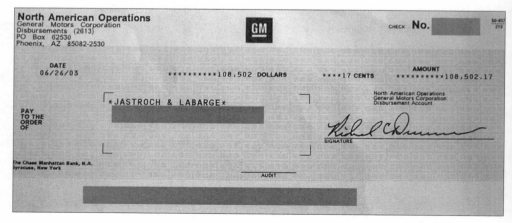

The check for the plaintiff's attorney fees as awarded by the court.

sure someone in Detroit must have an idea. General Motors wouldn't waste a quarter of a million dollars fighting over a $196 starting problem without a good reason. Would they? Nah....

The case tweaked the public's interest. The Associated Press sent the story across the wires. Radio talk show hosts came a callin'. The *National Law Journal*, *Lawyer's Weekly USA* and even Detroit's *Automotive News* reported on the decision. For a few days, my name was everywhere. Yes, GM certainly taught me a lesson.

The Losses

They say you can't win 'em all. Rocky Marciano did. Between 1947 and 1955, "The Rock" went 49 and 0 as a professional fighter. He retired as the only undefeated heavyweight champion of the world. Rocky Marciano won 'em all.

The Miami Dolphins were 17 and 0 in 1972. They are the only professional football team to have a perfect season. Oklahoma A & M was undefeated in 1946, 1947 and 1948 under legendary basketball coach Hank Iba. It might not be easy to win 'em all, but it can be done, for a while.

I am devastated when we lose. The agony of defeat is greater than the thrill of victory. I don't sleep. I don't talk. I don't eat. I only contemplate. Ninety-nine wins do not make one loss easier, for me or my client.

In 13 years, in 1,000 lawsuits, a jury has returned a verdict for Detroit 8 times. Where did I go wrong? What did I miss? Why didn't those 12 good people see it my way? We should NOT have lost the case. Maybe I'm in the wrong profession.

VW won a door lock case. Hyundai won a smelly car case. Ford beat us six times during the Attorney Brown hardball years and DaimlerChrysler persuaded a judge to dismiss a Magnuson-Moss case over engine carbon buildup BEFORE it went to the jury.

Still, its been a good record, if not perfect. I just have to keep reminding myself I'm not Rocky Marciano.

My Favorites

> *Roll down the windows, put down the top, crank up the Beach Boys, baby. Don't let the music stop. We're gonna ride it 'til we just can't ride it no more.*
>
> **— Randy Newman**
> *I Love LA*

Every case is special to me, every client unique. Each case has its own identity, its own story. No two are alike. When I first submitted this chapter to my publisher for consideration, it was 1,200 pages long. What you are about to read is the result of the "editing down" process. But make no mistake about it. ALL my cases are my favorites.

Tires for Your Lemon

I met Myron J. in July 1998, at Milwaukee's "Festa Italiana" — the largest Italian festival in America. I was hanging around listening to Danny and the Juniors, the 50s rock band. The leader, Joe Terri, was a *paisan* and still living, therefore meeting the only criteria to play at the Festa. That's where I bumped into Tony L. and his friend Myron. Tony was a client who had recently returned his lemon Plymouth Grand Voyager to the Chrysler Corporation. He and Myron were also enjoying the fireworks and mozzarella marinara.

After the customary *gumba* "How ya doin'?" greeting, Tony asked if I would talk to Myron about his car trouble. It seemed Myron was getting "vaffanculo" (the Italian runaround) from Oldsmobile. I said, "Of course I'll talk to Myron. Car trouble is my life." The three of us sat down, listened to a few choruses of *At the Hop*, and proceeded to badmouth the auto industry.

Myron told me that he bought a new Oldsmobile Ciera in September 1995. The car developed a vibration and shimmy. Myron was visibly concerned because the 3-year warranty was going to run out in two months. He had been talking with Oldsmobile, but was getting nowhere. Their best offer had been four new tires. I've never settled a claim for tires. A case would have to be pretty weak to settle for tires. I asked Myron to stop by my office with his paperwork.

The work history showed six repair visits for a shimmy/vibration concern, three during the first year, one in the second and two during the third year. We were one repair attempt short for the Lemon Law. Wisconsin requires four visits during the first year, but old Magnuson-Moss was still a possibility. As long as the repairs took place during the warranty period, Mag-Moss applied. I thought it would be worth writing to GM. Myron didn't have anything to lose.

On July 22, 1998, I sent a letter to General Motors seeking a replacement vehicle on behalf of Myron J. The letter was similar to hundreds sent by my office. However, this time the response came as a surprise: Ms. G. Rae Connor, a legal analyst with Oldsmobile, called Myron to share with him some of GM's "intimate" thoughts about me. She told Myron that I was just working for myself, didn't have my client's interest in mind, and had a "reputation" at her office. Concerned about what she said, Myron called me for an explanation.

I was livid. General Motors had offered my client FOUR TIRES, an offer that didn't even rise to the level of an insult. And I'm the scum? My client has to be warned about my reputation?

What? Did Ms. Connor think I was going to take two of the tires as a contingency fee?

We filed against General Motors Corporation on August 24, 1998. Four months later, on January 8, 1999, GM buckled. The case was settled. We accepted the four new tires, plus $5,700 in attorney fees. Maybe Ms. Connor was right. Maybe it is all about fees. Wait a minute... I forgot to mention one thing. The four new tires were attached to a new Oldsmobile.

"Grab Life by the Horns"

Commercials on Monday Night Football aren't cheap. Automotive advertising budgets explode trying to reach new buyers. Car dealers promise anything to pull customers into the showroom. Detroit is a vampire and consumers are the blood. So, why would DaimlerChrysler Corporation pay someone NOT to buy their product?

A client I'll refer to as Tom was only trying to take Chrysler's advertising advice. He wanted to "grab life by the horns." He wanted a piece of the American pie. With a new 2001 Dodge Ram 3500 SLT Cummins Turbo Diesel, Tom started his own business hauling cars across the United States. If you wanted a car delivered to New Orleans or picked up in Salt Lake City, Tom was your man. He was king of the road, logging 9,000 miles a month. There was one problem. Tom's Dodge Ram didn't work like the one described in the glossy Dodge Different promotional propaganda.

The Ram pictured in the brochure was the commercial truck of choice: "Because it works. And works. And works." Tom's didn't work. It died.

The red Dodge in the sales brochure was labeled: "**A genuine trucking legend**." Tom's Dodge should have been yellow and labeled: "**A genuine trucking LEMON**."

The promotional Ram had power, durability and efficiency, whether "hauling an RV over the Rockies, or hauling hay bales down on the farm." But Tom's Ram broke down hauling a Ford Escort to Des Moines.

At 57,000 miles, less than 5 months after delivery, Tom knew he had a lemon. He filed for arbitration with Daimler-Chrysler's Kangaroo Court — the National Center for Dispute Settlement. He explained that he had experienced major engine problems starting at 25,000 miles and attached 8 pages of related complaints.

The NCDS refused to hear the case. They said the non-conformity was an item "that is no longer in warranty" and "therefore, your situation falls outside the bounds of the arbitration process."

It bears repeating that Lemon Law arbiters are not lawyers. They are not trained in the technical analysis of legal terminology. Warranties can be sophisticated documents subject to myriad interpretations. Page 1 of Tom's 2001 Dodge Ram warranty booklet, for example, contains a chart showing warranty coverage. I have reviewed this chart very carefully and have concluded that Cummins diesel engine components ARE covered under warranty for 5 years or 100,000 miles.

If I am correct, the NCDS should not have turned Tom down. His claim was submitted five months after delivery with only 57,000 miles on the truck. He was well within the warranty coverage period. That's the way I read it, but I'll let you be the judge.

On the following page, you will find a copy of the "Warranty Coverage at a Glance" page from Tom's 2001 Dodge Ram Warranty Information booklet. Review the page to see if you think Cummins diesel engine components are covered under warranty for 5 years/100,000 miles. To be fair, I will give you the same clue given to all NCDS arbitrators. The eighth bar graph from the top addresses Cummins diesel engines. You may

Dodge Warranty Coverage

DESCRIPTION	1 Yr/ 12,000	2 Yr/ 24,000	3 Yr/ 36,000	3 Yr/ 50,000	3 Yr/ Unlimited	5 Yr/ 50,000	5 Yr/ 100,000	7 Yr/ 70,000	8 Yr/ 80,000	Lifetime
Basic Limited Warranty Coverage	■	■	■							
Special Extended Warranty Coverage										
Anti-Corrosion Perforation: All Panels	■	■	■	■	■					
Outer Panels	■	■	■	■	■	■				
Federal Emission Warranty — Light Duty Truck	■	■	■							
Federal Emission Warranty — Specified Components — Light Duty Truck	■	■	■	■	■	■	■			
California Emission Warranty — Light Duty Truck	■	■	■							
California Emission Warranty — Specified Components	■	■	■	■	■	■	■	■		
Cummins Diesel Engine Components (Including California Medium Duty Diesel Emissions)	■	■	■	■	■	■				
Federal Emission Warranty — Heavy Duty Truck	■	■	■							
Noise Emission Warranty — Heavy Duty	■	■	■	■	■	■	■	■	■	■

take up to 40 days to reach your conclusion, the same amount of time that "arbitration mechanisms" have to reach their decisions.

If your conclusion is that Cummins diesel engine components are covered under warranty for 5 years or 100,000 miles, you exceed the qualifications and brainpower necessary to become a Lemon Law arbitrator. To pursue an arbitration career, please feel free to contact:

> The National Center for Dispute Settlement
> 2777 Stemmons Freeway, Suite 1452
> Dallas, Texas 75207
>   *or*
> BBB Auto Line, Dispute Resolution Division
> 4200 Wilson Boulevard, Suite 800
> Arlington, Virginia 22203.

NCDS didn't see it my way or yours. Tom contacted my office. We sent a Lemon Law Notice to DaimlerChrysler seeking a replacement vehicle. Chrysler accepted our demand within 14 days. Tom turned in his 2001 Ram with 90,000 miles and received a new 2001 Ram with 33 miles. He continued hauling ass cross-country.

"Grab Life by the Horns" II

Wouldn't you know it? Tom's replacement Ram was just as bad as the original. Two months after delivery, one of "the longest-lasting full-size pickups on the road" — according to Polk Company, a leader in statistical automotive reporting — broke down on Interstate 40, southeast of Las Vegas, New Mexico. Another bad engine. The truck was towed 150 miles through the desert to the nearest Dodge dealer where they found metal particles in the oil.

The dealer recommended replacing the entire Cummins Diesel and Turbo Charger system because metal shavings had gone through the bearings. But Dodge was too cheap. They would only authorize a new "short block." Three weeks later they changed their mind and the Turbo was replaced in White-water, Wisconsin. Tom continued to have major engine problems. He made seven more trips to dealers and repair stops in Oklahoma City and Albuquerque. He also made another call to my office.

Tom's second Lemon Law Notice was mailed on April 12, 2002, about one year after returning Lemon I. Lemon II had 80,000 miles. DaimlerChrysler took issue with Tom's "business use" of the truck, despite their own promotional material, but agreed to replace it. However, they also strongly urged Tom to consider a refund in lieu of another Ram. The focus had shifted from customer satisfaction, to, "How in the hell do we get rid of this guy?" They decided to offer him an "incentive" to stay away.

Incentives such as rebates, cash back and owner loyalty cer-tificates are commonly used to promote sales and move inventory. Nobody in their right mind provides incentives to dis-courage customers. That goes against every fiber of Madison Avenue's being. Manufacturers don't pay people to NOT buy their product. Well, they did this time.

DaimlerChrysler wanted to get rid of Tom so badly they made him an offer he couldn't refuse. They agreed to refund all money dating back to Lemon I and write him an additional check if he promised to shop elsewhere. Tom accepted the offer. He didn't want to wake up with a ram's head in his bed. He further agreed that, "**neither he nor any member of his house-hold will purchase or lease any make or model of a vehicle manufactured by DaimlerChrysler**" for a period of ten years.

I believe Tom is still in business. I know the *Ford* Super Duty F-350 Power Stroke V8 Turbo Diesel is promoted as a tough and versatile commercial truck.

Make Mine to Go

In fall, 1994, the future client I'll call Matt drove past Soerens Ford, Home of the Nice Guys, in Brookfield, Wisconsin. He caught a glimpse of a Ford F-150 4-door pickup truck. This would be perfect for his growing family. In 1994, 4-door trucks were not common. F-150s were normally three-passenger, standard-cab pickups. The extended-cab craze was just beginning. Ford didn't even make an extended-cab F-150.

Through an arrangement with Centurion Vehicles of White Pigeon, Michigan, Ford sent standard F-150s to the Centurion factory to be cut in half and extended into six-passenger, 4-door crew-cab pickups. The truck that caught Matt's eye was such a conversion. On September 30, 1994, Matt laid out $27,990 for a new "hacked up" Ford crew-cab conversion.

Cruise control, brakes, transmission and pulling problems all surfaced within a few weeks. Before Christmas arrived, the Centurion conversion had spent 37 days in the shop. Before New Year's, Matt wrote a letter to Ford demanding a refund. Before the St. Valentine's Day Massacre celebration, we filed a lawsuit against Ford Motor Company.

This lawsuit took place during the hardball regime of Emperor James "*I don't give a shit*" Brown. Ford was less than sympathetic to Matt's concerns. According to Ford, Matt caused most of his problems by driving on paved mountain highways in Colorado — including I-25, I-70, I-76 — during a hunting trip. Apparently, the "Built Tough" advertising campaign doesn't apply to Denver streets or interstates. Centurion caused the other problems, according to Ford, by slicing the truck in half, even though Ford had authorized the cut.

I argued to the jury that Ford trucks have actually been seen on television climbing mountains and negotiating Bryce Canyon. Driving on a four-lane blacktop in Colorado Springs had to be less demanding than scaling the Grand Tetons. Likewise, the finger-pointing "Humpty Dumpty" defense aimed at Centurion was nothing but smoke. Ford's name was on the truck. Ford's warranty covered the truck. The consumer bought the truck at a Ford dealership. This lemon was Ford's responsibility. If Centurion had caused some of the problems, Ford could sue them.

The jury returned a plaintiff's verdict on January 13, 1997. Matt was entitled to $75,016.56, double damages plus interest. Ford promised to pay, but almost three months passed without payment. Judgment was entered against Ford on April 9, 1997, in favor of the plaintiff.

The great thing about hardball is that we get to play too. We gave Ford five days to pay the judgment. If we didn't have the money by then, WE would go after Ford. Five days came and went. No money.

On the sixth day, April 15, 1997, we filed six garnishment actions, five against separate Ford dealerships and one against Ford Motor Credit. If any of the parties had Ford vehicles on their lots or owed Ford money, they would be required to turn over the property and/or monies to the plaintiff, my client Matt, until his judgment was paid in full.

The garnishment actions proved quite effective. Ford didn't see any benefit in having sheriff deputies selling Mustangs at public auction in order to satisfy the outstanding judgment. Ford called saying they would give us the check as soon as we returned the lemon F-150. Of course, there was a snag.

The Home of the Nice Guys — the dealership who sold the truck — wouldn't let us back on the property. For some reason, they were unhappy with the handling of the case. Funny, I thought we had handled it quite well. Anyway, like in a 1940s spy movie, we would have to make the transfer of goods in some off-site setting. Hey, no problem. We are always pleased to accommodate our friends from Detroit.

The vehicle return was set up at a neutral location where over 100 billion have been served. The Ford rep, my client and my assistant Nancy, met at a local McDonald's Restaurant with Ronald as facilitator. Matt received $77,205, including interest; the Ford rep received a "lemon," and all parties opted for a Big Mac Value Meal. Everybody went away happy, or at least fed. But the story didn't end there.

Ford wouldn't pay the attorney fees of $78,000, so we fought. The Giant always puts up a good fight. This one would cost them. One year later, Ford paid us $102,000, the additional $24,000 due to the time we had to spend arguing over fees.

On Moral Grounds

I noticed nothing unusual about Steve G. when he walked into my office in January 2003. He was your typical consumer enquiring about his rights under the Lemon Law. Steve's Dodge Ram had a power-door-lock problem. The right rear-door lock was erratic. Sometimes it wouldn't lock; sometimes it wouldn't unlock. It took the dealer five tries over an eight-month period to fix it. Since the locks weren't fixed within four attempts, Steve had a decent case. I told him a full refund on his truck should be no problem. He wasn't interested.

Steve explained that morally he didn't feel it was fair to make Chrysler buy back his truck. He felt Chrysler owed him something for his trouble, but not $30,000. Steve was looking for about $6,000 in settlement.

I was very surprised. I'm used to clients wanting more, not less. I can remember only one instance where a client rejected a $30,000 offer from Isuzu and asked ME to make a counter offer for $25,000. My negotiation skills would surely be tested on this one. Whew! Isuzu accepted the counter offer without a fight.

Steve and I talked. He truly did not think it was fair to make Chrysler buy back his truck. I truly did not think it was fair to let Chrysler off the hook for six grand. Steve didn't want a refund. I didn't want $6,000. In fact, I told Steve I wouldn't take the case UNLESS we asked for a refund. We were at a friendly impasse. I had a suggestion. Let's test the Giant. (I knew they would fail, but Steve didn't. I wanted him to see for himself.)

I suggested that Steve take a couple of months and try to contact someone, ANYONE, at DaimlerChrysler who would listen to him. That itself would be quite an achievement. I told Steve to explain the whole story — his moral convictions, the fairness of $6,000, the strength of his case. See if anybody cared. This would give Chrysler the opportunity to satisfy their customer AND save money. If nothing happened, he could come back and we would go for the refund.

Guess what? Steve never got past customer assistance. His request to speak with a Chrysler zone manager or "higher up" was denied. When Steve told customer assistance that his attorney could get a refund in less than 30 days, customer assistance told Steve, "You better go back to that attorney, don't you think?" Steve did just that.

We faxed a Lemon Law Notice to DaimlerChrysler on April 8, 2003. Twenty-eight days later, Steve received a refund check in the sum of $30,083.33. Chrysler could have saved itself a lot of money had it just been willing to deal with a moral man. So much for morality in the Land of Giants.

No Defect Too Small

Give the American people a good
product, make it the right color,
and they'll buy it.

— **Lee Iacocca**
Former Chairman & CEO
Chrysler Corporation

Everybody thinks that when we talk lemon, we're talking only safety. Is the car dangerous? Does it stall in traffic? Did the brakes fail? Certainly, deathtraps must be bought back, but cars don't have to blowup to have an effect on their drivers. People don't have to be injured or die to prove a lemon. Lemon Laws involve much more than protection against disaster. Impairment of use and value also count, along with a lot of other things.

I'm very disappointed with consumer literature and Internet sites that claim Lemon Laws don't cover "minor problems." Even the usually reliable *West's Encyclopedia of American Law* has it all wrong. It states, "Paint defects, rattles, jumpy suspensions, and the like are not normally considered substantial defects." Not considered substantial by whom? My clients consider them substantial. Juries consider them substantial. I certainly do. I follow the Presumption of Nonconformity Rule — EVERY PROBLEM IS MAJOR UNTIL PROVEN OTHERWISE.

Detroit spends hundreds of millions of dollars each year selling us visions of automotive perfection. Those glossy ad cars don't rattle; those flashy television SUVs don't leak, even when being driven in the Colorado River. All I'm doing is asking the auto industry to live up to its promises. When the industry tells me that convertibles leak, doors rattle, pulling is normal, vibration can be expected, then I'll back off.

Until then, if some overpriced ad agency tells me I can climb the walls of the Grand Canyon or scale Mount Everest with my new Toyota 4 Runner, that Toyota better not shimmy on a flat stretch of Kansas highway. Herculean ads give rise to Herculean expectations.

Of course, even though people are paying that hefty 20 percent bite of after-tax income for new vehicles, they can't expect miracles on wheels. We all don't tear up mountains on a daily basis. But people certainly have the right to get what they are promised, the big things and the small.

Paint

If paint weren't important, every car would be beige. My first appearance in the Wisconsin Supreme Court involved paint and the Chrysler Corporation. I prepared 77 hours to make a 35-minute argument about paint scratches. I don't want to hear that paint isn't significant. Paint is important to every new car buyer. No exceptions!

Donna Hermes and Kerry Dieter signed a contract to purchase a new Dodge truck. The contract also provided for the purchase and installation of several after-market accessories, including a tonneau cover, bug deflector and fender shield. The accessories were all Chrysler-approved MOPAR parts. During the installation, the dealer scratched the paint finish in many places.

My clients tried to get out of the contract. The dealer forced them to take the Ram, promising to make it look like new. It never looked like new. We filed suit and found ourselves embarking on a five-year journey.

The trial court ruled against us. We appealed. The appellate court ruled against us. Our only chance now was to petition the Wisconsin Supreme Court and hope they'd take the case. Unlike the Court of Appeals, the Supreme Court doesn't have to grant every petition but can pick and chose the cases it will hear. Paint proved significant enough for the Supreme Court of Wisconsin. Our case was accepted.

The seven justices of Wisconsin's High Court handed down a unanimous decision. The Court reversed the two lower courts. Chrysler bought back my client's scratched up truck. It took five years, but we prevailed.

Drive = Love.

More Paint

New car buyers have a right to the same high gloss, satiny luster finish that appears on every vehicle pictured in every piece of promotional propaganda disseminated at car dealerships and auto shows across America. Lee Iacocca wouldn't accept fisheyes in his Dodge Viper. Why then should Thomas Claybon?

Thomas Claybon is an African-American who grew up in the South. At 15, he dropped out of high school to work on the family farm in Tennessee. He hasn't stopped working since. In 1977, Thomas moved to Milwaukee and started work in a steel factory. He met his wife, Jeanette. Seventeen years later, the Claybons bought their first house. Two years after that, they bought their first new car — a customized 1997 Chevy van.

The Astro came equipped with a $10,000 Coachman conversion package and a custom metallic paint job. Thomas put down a thousand hard-earned dollars and signed a seventy-two month finance contract. Payments were $515 a month, almost as much as the Claybon's house payment. They took delivery of their new van on a rainy June day and were told to bring it back the following week for a buff and a shine.

After the buff and shine, Thomas saw a problem. The van was covered with little dents. Something was wrong with the paint. It looked like dirt had gotten into the finish. Thomas talked to his salesman, William. Like all good salesmen, Bill said it was nothing. "We can buff this out. Just make an appointment." At the buffing appointment, the dealership confirmed the problem. The Claybon van was loaded with fisheyes.

Fisheyes is a trade term used to describe finish imperfection caused by silicone contamination. This happens when silicone is present on the surface of a vehicle not properly cleaned at the factory. Paint does not adhere to the silicone areas, leaving an uneven surface finish. Although it looks like dirt, a fisheye is more of a depression — a little dent.

The local Chevy dealer buffed the shit out of the Claybon van, but not the fisheyes. The van was sent back to the conversion company in Indiana. Maybe they had better buffers. They didn't. When the van was returned, the problem was worse. The fisheyes were still there and had now been joined by sand scratches and thin paint due to the relentless buffing.

The local dealer tried again and failed. Thomas and Jeannette were sick. Their new van was a mess. In all fairness, they wanted the van repainted. The dealer scheduled a meeting with the General Motors representative.

The GM rep was very helpful... to GM. Think about it. The GM rep represents GM. By his very title, that's his job. He works for GM. A GM rep can't act in the best interest of the consumer. That would be a conflict with the people who sign his paycheck. Can there be any doubt as to the outcome of the meeting?

General Motors would not authorize repainting the van. The $4,000 cost was too high. Besides, the van didn't need to be painted. So said the GM rep. As he told Mr. and Mrs. Claybon, there was "really nothing wrong with the van." He further claimed, "Most vans have a fisheye condition."

The insults to the Claybon's intelligence and dignity continued. The GM representative promised that with further effort, the van could PROBABLY be brought back to about 95 percent of what it should have been in the first place. GM would work with the dealer to attain this level of satisfaction. Then came the final punch — six inches below the belt. Mr. and Mrs. Claybon were offered $1,000 as "goodwill" for their inconvenience, for the loss of pride and pleasure they had taken in owning their first new vehicle. Jeanette broke down in tears.

On November 3, 1997, we filed a Lemon Law suit in Waukesha County, Wisconsin. It took nearly two years to bring the Philistine to its knees, but on July 1, 1999, a settlement was reached. Thomas and Jeanette Claybon kept the fisheye laden Astro van and were paid $25,000. In addition, GM and Coachman paid the attorney fees.

It seems to me that the defendants would have been much better off if they had just repainted the van as Mr. Claybon had requested. But what do I know?

Rattles

Dash rattles, door rattles and trunk rattles are certainly annoying, but do they rise to the level of nonconformities? Does a trunk or door rattle substantially impair the use, value or safety of the vehicle? Should the manufacturer be forced to buy back a car because the dash rattles? Frank S. thought so.

Frank S. was meticulous about cars, keeping his spotless, inside and out. He followed the Warren Buffett philosophy of automobile ownership — driving your vehicles at least ten years in order to minimize loss. In 1997, Frank sold his one-owner 1985 Chevy Celebrity and bought "America's Favorite Coupe," the Chevrolet Cavalier.

The 34-page Chevrolet brochure said its Cavalier was "raising the standard for small cars." The car was touted as an excellent choice for value, a "great car at a great price," one remarkable value with a "great ride!" Frank paid $13,675 in cash for the car and $988 for an extended warranty. If all went well, the new Cavalier would be parked in his garage until 2009.

All did not go well. Frank's Cavalier wasn't what it was cracked up to be — cracked being the operative word. The car shook, rattled and leaked. With less than 700 miles on the odometer, repair work began. It turned out that the dashboard had not been properly insulated. The dealer could hear creaking and cracking coming from the dash area, but wasn't sure of the cause or how to stop it. They tried foam.

The cruise control cable in the steering column was wrapped with foam tape. Foam was shoved into the back of the dash to stop a wire cluster from rubbing. The rattles continued. Two thousand miles later, screws were found missing in the dash. They were replaced. The rattles continued.

At 4,000 miles, the lower dash was insulated by jamming in more foam. The dealer thought MOVEMENT was causing the rattling. Brilliant! The rattles continued. One thousand miles later, more insulation was stuffed into the dash. The rattles continued. At 8,600 miles the dash cracked.

So much crap had been stuffed into Frank's dash that it burst apart. Styrofoam could actually be seen spewing from the seams. The entire dash panel had to be replaced. The rattles continued.

This "great car," at a "great price," with a "great ride," went back to the dealer four more times. They packed in more insulation and did more taping. The rattles didn't stop. On the tenth visit to the repair shop, Frank got the bad news. "Creaking panels are a characteristic of Cavaliers," he was told. Nothing more could be done.

The folks at the dealership told Frank that Cavalier dash panels are clipped together, causing flexing and bending when the Cavalier body moves. He'd be fine as long as the car was parked. No rattles then. But move the Cavalier and it would rattle. As a temporary fix, the dealer could lubricate the dash pad fittings. However, when the lubrication dried up, the noise would return. I suggested that Frank might consider carrying a can of WD-40 at all times. He could then oil the dash every few hundred miles. Frank didn't like my idea. He had one of his own.

Frank wanted to know if we could sue and get his money back. I told him I'd check the brochure to see if it mentioned the rattle-lube-dash condition. If General Motors had disclosed that all Cavaliers rattle and that dash lubrication was the only fix, though temporary, then I'd have to say "no" on a suit. They had given fair warning.

I read that brochure from cover to cover. Amazingly, there was no mention of lubrication, rattles, or multi-dash assemblies. I found no disclosures whatsoever relating to a dash rattle problem or any problem for that matter. There were, however, repeated references to value and greatness. TWENTY-ONE TIMES, the brochure talked about value, "exceptional value," "excellent value."

In my humble opinion, an exploding dash might be something remarkable, but it certainly can't be equated with value. Frank didn't get what GM promised. He got a rattling, foam-filled, always in need of lubrication, never-to-be-fixed dash. We sued General Motors and forced them to buy back "America's Favorite Coupe," foam and all.

Radios

I get really irritated when some lamebrain from Detroit tries to tell me that radio problems don't qualify under the Lemon Law. The defense mentality of, "It's only a radio. What do you expect us to do, buy it back?" doesn't work in Wisconsin. It doesn't work for me and it didn't work for Jennifer D.

Jennifer was a 24-year-old nursing school graduate. Not having much money, she had driven old beaters since high school. That was about to change. She was hired by Children's Hospital of Wisconsin. She could finally afford her dream car, a Pontiac Grand Am GT.

The Pontiac was jet black with chrome wheels, sunroof and factory upgraded stereo with surround sound. The radio would come in handy because Jennifer's job was 42 miles from home. Jennifer put $900 down and financed the balance. Her payments were $379 a month for 5 years.

From day one, the radio was a problem. The static was so loud and distracting that Jennifer couldn't play it. This was especially troublesome during her long daily commute. A brand new car, an upgraded stereo and SILENCE for that two-hour round trip. Sounds like a problem to me. It certainly doesn't match the "Fuel for the Soul" that Pontiac advertises, or the "We Are Driving Excitement" that Pontiac claims.

And while we're on the subject, why does every product in corporate America have to have a catchphrase attached to it? I don't want to "Grab Life by the Horns." I'm just trying to buy a Dodge. I don't know what "No Boundaries" means. WHAT is "Like a Rock?" Cadillac has made a "Break Through." So what? Big deal!

With Toyota, I "Get the Feeling." Thank you. Nissan is "Driven." Chevy claims, "We'll Be There," and Jeep sighs, "There's Only One." Thank God for that. We have carried "Wheaties, The Breakfast of Champions" much too far. Can't this society buy anything without some Madison Avenue slogan attached? But let's get back to Jennifer.

Pontiac dealers worked on Jennifer's radio for two years. They added ground wires to the firewall, ground wires to the wiring harness, installed filters, removed filters, exchanged radios, replaced radios, changed antennas, confirmed static, ticking and noise. They couldn't fix the problem. Twenty-three months and nine repair attempts after Jennifer took delivery of her dream car, the radio was actually worse. It stayed on between five and ten seconds after the car was shut off; an engine ticking noise came through the speakers and no matter how loud the music, the static was louder. Isn't this significant to an owner? Isn't this a lemon?

Jennifer sent a demand to General Motors. She asked for a refund because of all her radio problems. She was turned down. "General Motors can't buy back cars for every little thing. Radio problems are minor in nature. They don't rise to the level of nonconformity. They don't substantially impair use, value or safety." In essence, Jennifer was told to go to Radio Shack and pick up a portable if she wanted a radio in her car. We filed suit. Jennifer got her money back and GM got the car and the static.

Turn Signals

Dan C. was on his second or third lemon. I can't remember exactly. He sent me repair orders from Florida. His Chevy Cavalier was giving him trouble. The left turn signal wouldn't shut off automatically after wide turns. It just kept blinking. Dan would have to turn it off manually. Chevy dealers had checked it out, but couldn't find anything major wrong. The steering wheel just didn't turn back far enough to activate the automatic shut off. This was no big deal, or was it?

Dan's file sat around my office for six months. I wasn't sure we had a case. My Presumption of Nonconformity Rule — that every defect is major until proven otherwise — was being tested. The turn signal automatically shuts off most of the time. Did having to manually turn off a blinker give rise to a Lemon Law claim? Is this significant enough? What would a jury think? I called Dan to talk about substantial impairment.

Dan told me that he didn't always remember to turn off the malfunctioning blinker. He drove miles with the blinker signaling a turn he was never going to make. Motorists shouted obscenities as they passed. They flipped him "the bird." We know the scene. We've all followed some idiot on the highway with his blinker flicking away. It's frustrating because we don't know what the guy's going to do. But is that enough under the Lemon Law?

Then, Dan told me how he came close to having three accidents when on-coming drivers, thinking he was going to be turning left, turned in front of him. Okay, now I see the problem. That blinker signaled the potential of a future accident. That was substantial. I sent a notice to GM, who did the right thing. Within 30 days, Dan had a refund and Detroit had a car with leftist tendencies.

Keep Thinking Small

No, the automotive industry and I don't necessarily agree on what constitutes a substantial defect. I had that pointed out to me very clearly during the discussion phase of one of my cases. The finger pointer was another attorney, one representing the other side in a lemon case. We were meeting in a tiny office at a local car dealership.

The attorney verbally attacked my integrity. He accused me of having a reputation for taking small cases and making them into mountains. Again, I'm the scum. I shot back: "Don't ever question my integrity for representing people who get fucked by the auto industry. You and your client are the thieves. You are the scum. You are the lowlifes."

"We're outta here," I announced and started pushing Terry, my associate. We literally climbed over the attorney and the desk to get out of that office. I kept yelling all the way to the door, but have no recollection of what I said. The attorney was subsequently fired. Maybe he and his client thought the case was small potatoes, but my client and I never did.

Look, I don't deal in million dollar cases. I don't represent accident victims. I have never filed a class action lawsuit in my life. I represent the average Joe, the everyday man and woman who lives next door or down the street, the neighbor who lays down hard-earned cash for the privilege of driving a brand new car with a bumper-to-bumper warranty.

Detroit tells us that our cars are engineering marvels, masterpieces of design and performance, the finest technologically advanced motor vehicles ever put on the road. Like I said, I'm just making them live up to their promises.

Trunks shouldn't leak. Mirrors shouldn't vibrate. Doors shouldn't rattle. Heated seats should heat. Remote Keyless Entry systems should work. Dashboards should stay in place. Paint should shine. Radios should play. Blinkers should turn off automatically. And, when they don't, we go to court. It's that simple.

Nothing but the Facts

It was Tuesday, December fourteenth; it was windy in Los Angeles. We were working the day watch out of Bunco Division. A gang of petty swindlers had set up operations in the city. We had to stop them.

> **— Sergeant Joe Friday**
> *Dragnet*
> "The Big Betty," 1953

Sergeant Joe Friday was a straight-ahead "play it by the rules" LA cop. He fought crime in 1950's Los Angeles. Armed with sport coat, crew cut and tie, Joe took bad guys off the streets of television every Wednesday night in millions of living rooms across America. Mine was no exception.

As a kid, I liked those *Dragnet* nights. I looked forward to hearing the distinctive four-note intro and the classic opening: "Ladies and gentlemen, the story you are about to see is true. The names have been changed to protect the innocent." And then, Joe himself: "This is the city, Los Angeles, California. I work here. I'm a cop."

During the next 30 minutes a real-life story of crime, capture and conviction would unfold right before my eyes. Joe Friday taught me the importance of facts and what could be accomplished with knowing the facts. His methodical search for truth through the Socratic method of asking short succinct

189

questions and demanding equally succinct answers, never failed to protect the decent citizens of Los Angeles. Week after week after week, "Just the facts ma'am, just the facts," led to the arrest and conviction of countless evildoers.

When faced with your own trials and tribulations of owning a lemon, take a lesson from Sergeant Friday. Just as he put away the crooks of LA, you can slam the Giants of Detroit. Like Joe, what you need are the facts.

I can't overstress the importance of knowing, establishing and recording the facts of your case. You need to keep notes on WHO you talked to, WHAT was said and done and the WHERE, WHEN and WHY it all took place. You also need the HOWS — how your car's stalling problem affects its use, value and safety. Don't worry about complex legal theories or Johnny Cochrane type trial maneuvers. Leave that up to the lawyers. All you have to worry about are facts, "Just the facts ma'am, nothing but the facts."

The Telephone Call

During the time it takes to qualify your vehicle as a lemon, the telephone call probably occurs more often than any other event. Keep notes on every phone conversation relating to your vehicle. Whether you are talking to your salesman, a mechanic or the dealership's general manager, if it's about your car, **WRITE IT DOWN**. Write down the date, the time, what was said, who said it. **DOCUMENT ALL CALLS**. These notes become a reference when it comes time to prove what was said and when.

For example, if a service adviser calls and says, "I felt the front end shimmy during a test drive," your case has been bolstered. Their service adviser has become a key witness, FOR YOU! He can help you prove the fact that your car does vibrate. But what if he changes his tune? What if later he "doesn't remember" confirming the vibration? What if he doesn't remember you, the call or the car? It happens all the time.

Not to worry. Based on your notes, you will be able to specifically testify that on June 14, at 2:30 p.m. you had a telephone conversation with service adviser Mark Wilson who told you he felt the front end of your Pontiac Firebird shimmy during a test drive. Without the notes, your recollection would be nothing but guesswork, no more valid than that of the "forgetful" service adviser.

The Work Order

The work order is written by a dealership service adviser when a vehicle is dropped off for repair. This is the first documentation of your visit and your chance to describe your vehicle's problems in detail. **Take advantage** of this opportunity and give those details.

For example, if your car has a starting problem, don't say "I've had trouble starting my car." Explain how you were stuck in a parking lot waiting for roadside assistance or how you missed an important doctor's appointment because your car wouldn't start. Recount the number of times the car failed to start and how family members won't ride in it for fear of being stranded. The more descriptive the information on the work order, the better off you will be when it comes time to prove your lemon case.

"Customer states he was stranded two hours on country road when headlights stopped working," is compelling. "Check electrical," is not.

You have both the right AND the duty to give as much information as possible to assist the dealership in its repair efforts. Make sure your service advisor understands the severity of the situation and accurately records what you say. If the 'write-up' doesn't accurately reflect what you said, DON'T SIGN IT! Make the service adviser get it right.

Sometimes dealership personnel remember complaints that were never documented. I had one case where my client complained at every oil change that her Saab shook. Her concerns never appeared on any work order. I suggested she go back to the dealership and talk to the service adviser. If he remembered her complaints, she should get a note to that effect.

We ended up with a handwritten statement on dealer stationary that my client "had concerns with vibration at 1,842 miles and at every service visit since." What was an extremely weak case — if a case at all — became strong. We beat Saab with facts established through their own dealer's statement. Nice.

The Repair Order

The repair order, sometimes called the invoice, documents your visit to the shop. It contains your original concerns listed on the work order along with the corrective steps taken by the dealership. The more significant the repair, the more helpful the repair order will be in establishing the facts of your case. I don't like to see NPF (no problem found) or CND (could not duplicate) on repair orders. I do like "resurfaced warped front rotors" or "test drove vehicle and confirmed pull to left." **Specifics are powerful**.

You do have SOME control on what appears on the final repair order. Normally, a service adviser will go over the invoice with you when you pick up your vehicle. Advisers like to elaborate on the technician's work. They sometimes offer details that don't appear on the write-up. If the service adviser says something favorable to your case that is not on the repair order, ask him to add that information to the order. If he won't, you add it. Write down the date and exactly what was said and by whom.

In my son's Mustang case (Chapter 8), one repair order stated POO (parts on order) and nothing else. The service adviser told me not to take any long trips until the "special order" transmission part was installed. I immediately asked him to notate the repair order accordingly. He did. A future trial exhibit was then handed to me, warning: "Do Not Drive Extensively — Trans Leaking." What better proof of a defect than the defendant's own written instructions to limit use of the car due to a transmission leak.

Sometimes dealers don't want to give a repair order. They say, "We'll mail it," or "It's being held open," or "It's not ready." These excuses are NOT acceptable. You want something in writing TODAY showing the status of your car — not next week or next month or possibly never. Before you leave, you want written documentation from somebody at the dealership. I don't care if it's a handwritten note from the general manager or a sworn affidavit from the lot boy. **Get the proof!**

But what about those times when no repair order is issued? There are visits to the dealership when this happens. The dealer may look at your car, test-drive it, maybe even work on it without generating any paperwork. This kind of visit also counts when it comes to pursuing a Lemon Law case. Most state Lemon Laws only require that you make your vehicle available for repair, that you give the dealer a chance to fix it. If that opportunity doesn't produce paperwork, create your own.

Write down the date of the visit, the person or persons working with you, what was said and done. Include as many details as possible. It's a pretty good bet that no one at the dealership will remember anything about your visit. Your notes can be used to prove facts that otherwise would be lost.

Days Out of Service

One way to win a Lemon Law case is to show that a vehicle was "out of service" for a specific number of days, usually 30. Once 30 days are established, you have a good case. However, don't rely on dealership repair orders to establish days out of service. Repair orders are notoriously wrong.

I've seen the dates on repair orders off by a day or two and I've seen them off by months. Usually the date you drop your vehicle off is correctly stated on the order because *most* service advisers can type in Today's Date. The date you pick it up is another story. Once again, it's up to the consumer to take control.

When you pick up your vehicle, check the date on the repair order. If it's wrong, ask that it be corrected. And, as further protection, keep your own record of Days Out of Service. All you need to do is mark on your calendar the day you take your car to the shop and the day you pick it up. It sounds rather simplistic but it gives you proof of the Days Out of Service from your own records. You won't have to rely on the dealer's inaccurate repair orders.

The Repair Visit

Another way to win a Lemon Law case is to establish that a specific nonconformity was not repaired within a specific number of attempts, usually three or four. This seems pretty straightforward, but manufacturers and dealers count to four differently than consumers.

If I take my car in for brake work and the dealer has to order parts, two scenarios are presented. If the dealer keeps my car until the parts come in, that's one repair attempt. If the dealer doesn't keep my car and says bring it back when the parts come in, that's two repair attempts in most states. However, dealers and manufacturers like to argue that the second scenario is only one repair attempt because it relates back to the first visit. Don't let them feed you this line!

Every time you take your car in, every time you make it available for repair — regardless of what the dealer does, OR DOESN'T DO — that visit counts. Keep track of these repair visits. Don't rely on the dealer or manufacturer. They have that funny way of counting.

Technical Services Bulletins

You may remember the story earlier in the book about the Chevy truck with an engine knock that wouldn't quit. The dealership explained it away with a Technical Service Bulletin. Issued by General Motors, the TSB stated that this cold start engine knock was a condition found in their 1999–2002 trucks.

There are TSBs on every car. They provide dealership personnel with excuses as well as diagnostic and corrective information. They also establish facts for the consumer from the manufacturers' own documents.

Get copies of **ALL** Technical Service Bulletins relating to your vehicle. If your dealer won't supply them — and they probably won't — go to the Internet: www.alldata.com is a good source. Pay special attention to the bulletins that apply specifically to your problems, but don't overlook the others. You may find defects you didn't know you had.

I'll never forget pulling up an astonishing 170 Technical Service Bulletins for a client's 1999 Mercury Cougar V-6. I couldn't get K. C. Douglas' song out of my head:

> *If I had money, I'll tell you what I'd do,*
> *I'd go downtown and buy a Mercury or two,*
> *I'm crazy 'bout a Mercury,*
> *I'm gonna buy me a Mercury and*
> *Cruise it up and down the road.*

The Photograph/Video

A picture is still worth a thousand words. Take a photograph of anything that helps prove a fact in your case — the smoking engine, being jumped by roadside assistance, your truck on a flatbed. Stating, "My truck has an oil leak," isn't persuasive. An 8" x 10" glossy of your slimy oil-stained driveway is.

I took 108 pictures in my Corvette case. The prize photo showed three Chevrolet technicians lying underneath my car trying to figure out why the rear end clunked. GM never saw that picture. The case settled too quickly. But I was ready. You must be too.

If a picture is worth a thousand words, a video is worth ten thousand words or possibly dollars. **IF THE PROBLEM CAN BE VIDEOTAPED, VIDEOTAPE IT**. Blue smoke coming from the tail pipe, a violent shake, water leaking through the convertible roof are facts that can be proven with videotape. And what's even better, it's your camcorder. If at first you don't succeed, erase and try again.

Keep It All

I am amazed by the number of people who throw away important papers. I keep everything. I don't like hearing clients say, "I didn't know I was going to have all this trouble. Had I known, I would have kept better records."

Of course, we would all adjust our behavior today if we knew what was going to happen tomorrow. I would have sold Lucent Technologies, or never bought it in the first place, had I known it was going to drop from $88 a share to $1.68.

Since you can't see a lemon lawsuit in your future, you must keep everything — rental contracts, appointment cards, phone messages, letters, notes, calendars — anything and everything that relates in any way to your car problems. You never know when it will come in handy. Be like Kim Shendel.

Kim's Calendar

No one I have ever represented took better notes than Kim Shendel. She and her husband John bought a new 1994 Pontiac Bonneville. Three months after delivery they noticed the windshield wipers only worked on the high speed setting. The Shendels immediately drove to a Pontiac dealer who confirmed the problem. As might be expected, no repair order was generated at this first visit, but an appointment was scheduled. Kim wrote everything down on her monthly planner.

Before the scheduled appointment, the wipers stopped working during a rainstorm. Kim notated her calendar and called the dealer. The wipers malfunctioned two more times before the appointment. Both times were documented on her calendar. Finally the appointment date arrived and a new wiper motor was installed. When Kim left the dealership, the wipers didn't work at all. She immediately drove back and left the car.

At this point, Kim had only one written repair order. But she had made three trips to the dealership, called once, and had a sum total of six entries on her calendar.

This pattern continued over the next several months. Kim made 17 more calendar entries and 11 more trips to the repair shop. She received another dealer invoice and now had a total of 14 visits to dealers, numerous phone calls, and 23 entries on her calendar. Concerned about their own safety, the Shendels wouldn't drive the Bonneville if rain was in the forecast.

Another seven months passed. Calendar notations numbers 24 through 39 were recorded. Seven additional repair visits occurred. Three additional dealership repair orders were written.

After 21 repair opportunities, a Lemon Law Notice was sent to General Motors. It was rejected. Apparently, nothing in this almost yearlong saga seemed substantial to GM. We filed.

At Kim Shendel's deposition, General Motors discovered the most incredible documentation of defective Pontiac windshield wipers since the invention of the blade. GM's attorney flew back to Minneapolis, called my office and settled the case for almost double the purchase price. Kim's calendar of facts beat the Giant. Joe Friday would be proud.

The Facts

PREPARING FOR BATTLE

Telephone Calls
Keep written records of dates, time, names.
Take notes on all conversations.

Work Orders
Give details of vehicle problems
and how the problems affect you.
Make sure your concerns are noted.

Repair Orders
Check accuracy, including dates.
Work with service adviser in making the information specific.
Add any comments supportive of your case.

Repair Visits
Make notes on all visits to dealerships,
relative to vehicle problems.

Personal Calendar
Keep a calendar of visits to
dealerships, days the car is kept for repair, and
other events related to the potential lemon.

Photographs/Videos
When possible, keep a visual record
of your vehicle problems.

KEEP COPIES OF EVERYTHING!

Closing Thoughts

A GM attorney once asked me, "You know how we could put you out of business?"

"No," I said. "Hire Sammy the Bull?"

"By building better cars," he replied.

Yeah, I thought, that would do it. I've only sued Toyota four times in thirteen years and the Camry is one of the best selling cars in America — **#1** for five of the last six years. If every manufacturer followed Toyota's lead, you could find ME begging in the yellow pages for one-third of your personal injury claim, or worse yet, selling cars. But until Detroit builds those better cars, I plan to be right here.

I am fortunate to live and practice law in Wisconsin, a state where Lemon Law justice thrives. In Wisconsin, the auto industry is punished for making crap and not taking it back. In Wisconsin, the consumer can stand toe-to-toe with Detroit. Residents of other states are not so fortunate.

Seventy-five million Americans live in states where Lemon Laws are so useless — so biased in favor of Detroit — that they might as well be repealed. Seventy-five million Americans do not have Lemon Law protection. In these states, just like customer assistance helpfully tells you, Detroit does NOT buy back cars. The auto industry is big business and big business gives nothing unless forced. Without effective Lemon Laws, today's consumer is no better off than the car buyer of 1945 who was told to drive to Detroit for repairs.

It is time for states with weak and ineffective Lemon Laws to step up to the plate and go to bat for the consumer. Playing ball with Detroit must end. I challenge the Honorable Kathleen Sebelius, Governor of Kansas, to step forward and say, "Our Lemon Law sucks. Let's do something about it."

I challenge Attorney General Lisa Madigan to be outraged by Illinois' pitiful excuse at automobile consumer protection. I challenge the Honorable Bill Owens of Colorado to admit that he is embarrassed to be governor of the state with the worst Lemon Law in America. I challenge all politicians from states with terrible Lemon Laws to make changes. Seventy-five million consumers desperately need your help.

Consumers go through Hell when they get stuck with a lemon. First they have the frustration of the lemon itself. Then they have the even greater frustration of dealing with Detroit. It is no wonder irate consumers paint their lemons yellow, picket dealerships and drive cars through showroom windows. It's not that these people are crazy. They just don't know where to turn. And the one industry they can turn to "doesn't give a shit."

I am furious with this industry! Whether it's the dealership, customer assistance, the regional rep, or LEE IACOCCA himself, the automotive industry is geared to deny. This industry unashamedly continues to lead consumers down the path of no recourse. Too often the bottom line is all that matters. Why spend $11 to make a car safer by moving the gas tank? That's not good business. Let people burn!

The one thing I've learned from my clients over the years is that they desperately need help in fighting the auto industry. Consumers are lost, and incapable of taking on Detroit alone. No matter how "consumer friendly" Lemon Laws may seem, no matter how many "independent" arbitration boards exist, no matter how many web sites pop up trying to offer guidance, going after Detroit on your own is vehicular suicide!

Lemon Law justice cannot be obtained by filling out some form from the BBB or calling your state Lemon Law administrator. Lemon Law justice cannot be obtained by talking to your salesman, or anyone else at the dealership. Lemon Law justice is gained through battle. And, for this battle, you do need a lawyer.

In America, there is no shortage of lawyers. In fact, there may be a glut. I am still amazed by the number of personal injury attorneys advertising on TV. How can all these lawyers make a living? (We could rid ourselves of half the lawyers in America if people simply learned how to drive.) But when it comes to automobile warranty law, attorneys are often nowhere to be found.

I looked through the Attorneys section of the Dallas, Texas, Yellow Pages. Out of 118 pages of lawyers, not one Magnuson-Moss or Lemon Law ad appeared. And the population of greater Dallas is 3.6 million. The story's the same in St. Louis, Miami and Tucson. For whatever reason, there is an obvious shortage of attorneys willing to take on Detroit. I'd like to see that change.

For My Fellow Lawyers

We need good Lemon Law lawyers. We need good Magnuson-Moss lawyers. I would like to encourage attorneys who care about consumer protection — who care about the little guy — to learn more about these laws. From talking with many of you around the country, I know you have the interest. I know you have the passion. It's just a matter of becoming familiar with these areas of law and putting your passion to work. It will pay off — for you and your clients.

You can make a good living representing consumers in their battles with Detroit. Consumers need sound legal advice in the world of the automotive warranty. They need your help. Give it to them. Don't be afraid of Detroit. When the man said, "The bigger they are, the harder they fall," he wasn't just talking about Paul Bunyan. The Giants of Detroit fall too. And when they do, the pay-off is big.

If your state has a good Lemon Law, use it. It will be your best weapon against Detroit. If you practice law in Texas or Oklahoma or some other state with a good-for-nothing Lemon Law, file your claims under Magnuson-Moss.

In 1995, I didn't know the first thing about Mag-Moss. Now we use it all the time. It works. If we can nail Detroit in Wisconsin, you can nail them in Nevada and North Dakota. Nissans are Nissans, no matter where they're "Driven." All you have to do is know the law and believe in your case.

For My Fellow Consumers

Traditionally the consumer's battle with Detroit has been difficult — at times seemingly impossible. The industry is mighty, made up of the most powerful corporations on earth. Consumers are small, microscopic in comparison. It's no wonder that the "little guy" has historically backed down when faced with the prospect of going up against the Giant. This need no longer be the case.

Don't be scared off by the auto industry. Don't be intimidated. If your car has problems — if it's a lemon — fight for your rights. Don't throw in the towel just because Detroit turns you down. Stand your ground. There are laws in place that give you the necessary ammunition to go after Giants. You can be the aggressor. You can be David. You can win the battle.

For My Clients

I have been privileged over the years to represent many wonderful people in their battle for Lemon Law Justice. Often these people were at their wit's end, on the verge of giving up. I am humbled by their courage. They did not give up, did not quit. They had the strength and faith to dig in and join me in battle. Together we toppled many Giants. For this I am grateful.

Without my clients, there would be no stories, no victories, no accountability in Detroit. Without my clients there would be no Lemon Law Justice.

Epilogue

So David prevailed over the
Philistine with a sling and with
a stone, and struck the Philistine,
and killed him.

— **I Samuel 17:50**
King James Version of the Bible

Acknowledgements

First and foremost, I would like to acknowledge my clients, each and every one of whom gave me the privilege of representing them in their battle against Goliath. Without them, this book would not have been possible.

I'd like to thank Ken Graun at Ken Press for his unending support and commitment to this project. He truly understands the battle, and why *Goliath* had to be published. He is a small but mighty publisher — the perfect match for this work.

I'd like to acknowledge the Lemon Law team at Jastroch & LaBarge: William S. Pocan, attorney extraordinaire; Susan Grzeskowiak, co-counsel (we nailed them in *Megna, Sr.*); Nancy Haselwood, for returning more lemons than the state of Texas; Debbie Hemauer, for being the best secretary ever; Sharon Baewer, for sending out more than 450,000 brochures. And the non-lemon law team (for listening to all my Lemon Law stories and feigning interest): Leonard Jastroch, Gerald LaBarge, Karen Appel, Jean Brown, Lisa Holahan, Pamela Wiza, Linda Arend, Janice Limbach, Craig TeLindert, Joanne Nordstrom, Casey Van Ark, Michelle Kollath, Maria Lovdal, Stephanie Shaver, Noreen Zahn, and Mike Ledzian.

My special thanks to Kathleen Walker, editor-in-chief, for helping me find my voice. Without her I'd still be talking in the first, second and third person in every sentence.

Additionally, thank you Todd Gadtke for being a friend and colleague fighting for Lemon Law justice in Minnesota. Also, many thanks Gary Heidenreich for your creative support.

I appreciate my friendship with Ed Henry over the past few years. Thank you for your invaluable contributions.

And finally, thanks and love to Connie, my wife, Chris, our son, and my parents for their contributions to my life and to this book. Without Connie's help, I'd still be writing the "Kangaroo Courts of Arbitration." I worked on that chapter for three straight months. Then I asked for help. Connie read the chapter. The next day she explained the errors of my ways, and gave me a two-page Kangaroo outline. So simple.

Chris was my first editor — he liked my book. He says I should go to Austin, Texas to talk about improving the Texas Lemon Law and getting rid of the death penalty.

My father's case against GM was the most important case of my life. My dad put me through law school and bought me my first Chevy Impala. I could NOT lose his case! No matter what! And so we had a great time fighting the Giant.

APPENDICES

State by State Rating
of Lemon Laws

Lemon	◯
Weak	★
Average	★★
Good	★★★
Outstanding	★★★★

ALABAMA ★★

I like the band, but I won't drive on George Wallace Boulevard. The law is average.

ALASKA ◯

The winter is too dark. No attorney fees to a prevailing consumer.

ARIZONA ★★★

Good consumer protection; one of the few states with a used car Lemon Law.

ARKANSAS ★★★

Bill Clinton did above average — at least in Arkansas.

CALIFORNIA ★★★★

You gotta love the state that ordered a 45-day suspension of Chrysler's license to sell vehicles because it laundered lemons.

COLORADO ◯

The only state that requires the consumer to pay the manufacturer's attorney fees if the consumer loses. This law was drafted in Dearborn, Michigan.

CONNECTICUT ★★

State run arbitration is binding. If you lose, it's over. But state run arbitration is OPTIONAL. I'd skip it.

DELAWARE ★★
Average consumer protection.

DISTRICT of COLUMBIA ◯
The Board of Consumer Claims Arbitration consists of 7 members appointed by the Mayor. Too political — I wonder why? No attorney fees if consumer sues manufacturer.

FLORIDA ★
I love Disney World, but hate the Florida Arbitration Board.

GEORGIA ★
Too much like Florida.

HAWAII ◯
If you appeal a non-binding arbitration award and don't improve your position by 25 percent, you pay the manufacturer's attorney fees.

IDAHO ★★
Average consumer protection.

ILLINOIS ◯
How can the land of Lincoln and Michael Jordan give us such a piss poor law? No attorney fees to a prevailing consumer.

INDIANA ★★★
I like John Mellencamp and the Indiana Lemon Law.

IOWA ★★★
Good consumer protection. If the manufacturer appeals a state-certified arbitration decision in bad faith, the consumer gets double, and possibly triple the award.

KANSAS ◯
The band was okay if you like corporate rock. No attorney fees to a pre-vailing consumer.

KENTUCKY ★
The birthplace of Abe Lincoln, Muhammad Ali and Loretta Lynn should do better than this.

LOUISIANA ◯

90 days out of service to qualify for relief is absolutely ludicrous.

MAINE ★★★

This is a good law. 15 business days out of service qualifies for relief. Too bad there's state run arbitration.

MARYLAND ★★★

You can go straight to court. Arbitration is optional. Camden Yards is a great ballpark.

MASSACHUSETTS ★★

Arbitration is optional, double damages possible. Consumers do better than the Red Sox.

MICHIGAN ★★

Not too bad, considering it's the home of Detroit. Be careful of mandatory arbitration, however, if you work for the auto industry.

MINNESOTA ★★★

Jesse Ventura wasn't too bad after all.

MISSISSIPPI ★

I am not a fan of Trent Lott, but I love BB King. The 20 cents per mile usage charge is too high.

MISSOURI ◯

If you file suit, and don't recover 10 percent more than was offered prior to filing suit, you MUST pay the manufacturer's attorney fees.

MONTANA ◯

Why doesn't Evel Knievel's home state cover motorcycles? No attorney fees to a prevailing consumer.

NEBRASKA ★★

Warren Buffett's state could do better.

NEVADA ◯

You'd think that a state with legalized prostitution could come up with a better Lemon Law. No attorney fees to a prevailing consumer.

NEW HAMPSHIRE ★
About the same as its neighbor, Vermont. Too much arbitration.

NEW JERSEY ★★★★
You can go straight to court. Arbitration is optional. I like The Boss.

NEW MEXICO ★
If you file a Lemon Law claim, you can't file a UCC claim. Why not?

NEW YORK ★★★
Good consumer protection *includes* used car Lemon Law.

NORTH CAROLINA ★★★
Treble damages to the consumer if the manufacturer unreasonably refuses to comply with the Lemon Law. I like it.

NORTH DAKOTA ◯
Fargo is one of my favorite movies. But son of a gun, why the heck is this here Lemon Law so weak, yahh?

OHIO ★★★★
The consumer does not pay a mileage/usage charge, whether refund or replacement. Is Pete Rose ever going to get into the Hall of Fame? What are the odds?

OKLAHOMA ◯
The corn may be as high as an elephant's eye, but the Lemon Law sucks. No attorney fees to a prevailing consumer.

OREGON ★
The Lemon Law allows treble damages. That's good. But if the consumer loses, the court MAY order consumer to pay the manufacturer's attorney fees. That's bad!

PENNSYLVANIA ★★
Average at best. The Lemon Law coverage period is too short — one year/12,000 miles.

RHODE ISLAND ★★
It may be small, but RI has done a lot better than Texas.

SOUTH CAROLINA ★★
Not bad for a state with such a flag problem.

SOUTH DAKOTA ★★
Much better than North Dakota. I like Mount Rushmore.

TENNESSEE ★★
The home of Elvis and Sun Records must do better.

TEXAS ◯
Arbitration is crazy here. No attorney fees to a prevailing consumer.

UTAH ◯
Court MAY award attorney fees to the prevailing party. Not as bad as Colorado, but bad enough.

VERMONT ★
Vermont loves its state run arbitration program. I don't.

VIRGINIA ★★★
Treble damages are possible. Arbitration is optional. I like Virginia — *Only the Good Die Young*.

WASHINGTON ★★
Too much arbitration.

WEST VIRGINIA ★★
Not as good as Virginia.

WISCONSIN ★★★★
If all Lemon Laws were like Wisconsin, Detroit would make better cars. Double damages if the Giant doesn't pay up within 30 days of demand.

WYOMING ★★
Average consumer protection. Gerry Spence could make it better.

Resources

www.lemonlawjustice.com
My site that supports *Bring On Goliath*. Includes general Lemon Law information and resources.

www.autopedia.com
The Automotive Encyclopedia. Includes full text of each state Lemon Law, Magnuson-Moss Warranty Act. Links to research, pricing, dealers, manufacturers.

www.carlemon.com
Lemon law summaries and statutes for each state.

www.alldata.com
Comprehensive automotive information. Includes access to Technical Service Bulletins and Recalls for all vehicles.

www.nhtsa.com
National Highway Traffic Safety Administration. Regulates the motor vehicle industry. Provides information on vehicles, equipment, safety, crash tests, recalls, bulletins, consumer complaints.

www.autosafety.org
The Center for Auto Safety. Strong consumer group that speaks out on auto safety and reliability.

www.edmunds.com
Guide to new and used car pricing — MSRP and invoice. Reviews, tips, discussions.

www.carfax.com
Vehicle history reports on used vehicles, including lemon check, accidents, odometer fraud.

www.jaslaw.com
Jastroch & LaBarge, SC. Where I practice Lemon Law.